PIOMINKO

CHICKASAW LEADER

To the Tate Family,
wishing you the best.

Mitch Caver

Thomas W. Cowger | Mitch Caver

ISBN: 978-1-935684-53-4

Book & Cover Design: Hannah Waggoner
Cover Illustration: James Blackburn

Chickasaw Press
PO Box 1548
Ada, Oklahoma 74821

www.chickasawpress.com

TABLE OF
CONTENTS

FOREWORD

by GOVERNOR BILL ANOATUBBY

PIOMINKO worked his way up from among the ranks of the Chickasaws' eighteenth-century warriors to become regarded as a trusted and respected leader and diplomat during and after the turbulent years while the British colonies became the United States. The decisions he made and the actions he took, sometimes with and sometimes against many well-known names of early US history, were critical to the survival and sovereignty of our people.

Paying tribute and respect to Piominko as a leader and an ancestor is a custom in the Chickasaw Nation. We go to lengths to educate our citizens about him. Many scholarly articles have told parts of his story in our *Journal of Chickasaw History and Culture.* An exquisite sculpture of Piominko was installed in 2014 on the grounds of the Chickasaw National Capitol Building in Tishomingo, Oklahoma. In 2010 we inducted him into our Hall of Fame. And we honor him with a national holiday observed on the second Monday of each October. Other Americans have also paid tribute to Piominko's achievements and importance. For example, another striking statue of him can be found outside the city hall in Tupelo, the historic town near his homestead in our Homeland in Mississippi.

Piominko: Chickasaw Leader tells for the first time his whole story and teaches us how crucial his leadership was during some of history's most uncertain and dangerous times. The authors of this important work, Thomas Cowger and Mitch Caver, have dedicated much of their lives to learning and telling about Native and Chickasaw history and culture.

Mitch Caver is a native of Baldwyn, Mississippi, a town very close to the center of our people's Homeland. Mitch has for many years been a great friend of the Chickasaw Nation. Since he was a boy he has appreciated the importance of the history of the land where he lived, and of our unconquered and unconquerable people who lived there before him. Often he toiled to uncover records and artifacts that revealed previously unknown information about the lives of our past leaders and ancestors. We have gratefully recognized his dedication to the enhancement of the knowledge of Chickasaw history with the Friend of the Chickasaw Award and honorary citizenship in our Nation.

Professor Thomas Cowger has held the Chickasaw Nation Endowed Chair in Native American Studies at East Central University in Ada, Oklahoma, for more than a dozen years. His achievements within the ECU scholarly community, and especially on behalf of Native students and research, have been important to the present renaissance of histories and cultures of many tribes, particularly ours. Tom's influence and impact reach across Indian Country and throughout the academic realm of Native studies. Since before earning his master's degree and a doctorate in history from Purdue University in the late 1980s and early '90s, he has been a determined leader in the investigation and revelation of the story of Native people from our point of view.

In *Piominko: Chickasaw Leader*, Mitch and Tom combine their experience, resources, and enthusiasm for history to produce this groundbreaking book. We are grateful to them for joining us in the courageous task of telling the stories that enrich our appreciation of Chickasaw heritage and support our commitment to sharing our story with the world.

PREFACE

DURING a heavy rain in Tupelo, Mississippi, in August 2013, I explored several important sites connected to the prominent Chickasaw leader Piominko and became more fully introduced to him and his legacy. I was traveling through the Chickasaw Homeland in Mississippi with Chickasaw students from East Central University. I visited Piominko's former village site, and the area where many believe he is buried. Brad Lieb, Ph.D., director of archaeology and field study for the Chickasaw Nation, skillfully led the tour and provided a brief overview of Piominko's life and historical significance. When I asked him whether a biography existed about Piominko, I was astonished to learn not only was the answer no, but that little had been written about him. I decided his important story needed to be told.

On the same trip I discovered Mitch Caver had been researching Piominko for nearly a decade in preparation for writing a book on the Chickasaw leader. I had met Mitch a couple of years earlier on a previous trip to the Homeland, and we had also corresponded a few times about Chickasaw boarding schools. Mitch, a lifelong Mississippian, grew up hearing stories about Piominko and knew all the places named after him. However, he knew most in his state knew little about Piominko or the rich Chickasaw history in the region.

Soon after, Mitch and I decided to combine our resources and write Piominko's story. We hope it has proven to be a successful collaboration between a professionally trained historian and published author, and a "Friend of the Chickasaws" with an extensive knowledge of and insatiable interest in Chickasaw history in the Homeland, particularly about Piominko. We brought different but complementary skill sets to the task. Not only has our collaboration produced a book, but it also has given us a terrific friendship.

Our journey of collecting and organizing materials and writing has taken us nearly four years. It has not been without difficulties. Despite Piominko's immense importance in Chickasaw and American history, the written secondary and primary sources on him are sparse, and the oral histories almost non-existent. Relevant pages about Piominko in James Atkinson's *Splendid Land, Splendid People* and Colin Calloway's *The American Revolution in Indian Country* provided a broad overview of Piominko's life and a nice starting point.

In order to depict him as fully as possible, we had to piece together as much information as we could find from a variety of sources and try to weave those threads together. We hope we did him justice, but at the same time we realize that there are some areas of his life we simply do not know, and there are questions surrounding him we cannot answer because of the lack of historical evidence. It is our hope that with the passage of time sources will emerge to help fill those gaps.

Wherever possible we tried to add as much of a Chickasaw perspective to the story of Piominko and his times as the sources allowed, as limited in type and availability as they were. We also had to try to read past the biases of the people who left the records. The same can be said for fleshing out details about his personal traits and personality. In the absence of a personal diary, log, or oral histories, we were left to rely on what others said about him. Fortunately, many specialists at the Chickasaw Nation and elsewhere helped us fill in some of the holes and shaped our understanding. Anytime we could use Piominko's own words, even though transcribed by someone else, we did.

As we began collecting the primary sources, we were struck by two things. First, Piominko had an absolutely unwavering commitment to a set of principles that guided his every decision. These were his passionate defense of Chickasaw sovereignty, his vehement refusal to sell Chickasaw lands, and his fervent belief that a Chickasaw alliance with America represented the best hope for a prosperous future for both nations and for later generations. He never veered from his positions, even at times when his stance placed him in great peril. Second, we noticed how incredibly well-known nationally he was during his lifetime. In retrospect, there was good reason for that. Arguably, without Piominko's resolute support of America while it was in its infancy, the United States could easily have lost the Southeast to Spain. Moreover, the Cumberland Valley region would never have been settled as quickly, nor would states like Tennessee and Kentucky arisen as fast. Thus, not only was Piominko a Chickasaw leader who vigorously promoted the autonomous rights of his nation, but he was also a loyal friend to America. This country owes him a debt that is immeasurable and virtually impossible to repay.

His historical significance cannot be overstated, and we are left wondering what course American history may have followed without Piominko's leadership at that critical time. His rise from a relatively unknown warrior to the consensus leader of the Chickasaw Nation whom President George Washington entertained in the President's House in Philadelphia bears resemblance to a movie script. He was not only a war leader with few equals, but an extraordinary visionary. His contemporaries over two centuries ago readily recognized his numerous accomplishments and paid tribute to him with plans for cities and place names, and may have even commissioned a renowned sculptor to carve a ship's figurehead in his likeness. We felt it time to resurrect his story for new generations and to restore his significant place in history.

In the process of researching, writing, and publishing this book we owe a debt of gratitude to multiple individuals and institutions. First and foremost, we are thankful for the support of Chickasaw Nation Governor Bill Anoatubby, who in a real sense is a visionary himself, much like Piominko. He has defended and promoted Chickasaw sovereignty and led the Chickasaw Nation through a period of unparalleled growth, in which Chickasaw fires are burning stronger than ever. We are also grateful for the assistance of Chickasaw Nation's Secretary of Culture and Humanities Lisa John, who encouraged the project from the beginning, and who has a personal affinity for Piominko. Chickasaw Nation Director of Research and Cultural Interpretation LaDonna Brown generously provided critical and invaluable insights about Chickasaw names and titles, Piominko, and the times in which he lived. Brad Lieb provided timely guidance and encouragement. Language and research consultant John Dyson patiently endured numerous requests from us to translate words from Chickasaw to English and to answer culturally related questions. John's fine book, *The Early Chickasaw Homeland: Origins, Boundaries and Society*, helped to shape this one. We are thankful to conservator Mark Adams for his exceptional willingness to provide photos and an immense amount of detail relating to the figurehead mentioned in chapter 5, and for his willingness to ensure that we told its story accurately. We are appreciative of Rick Thompson, a senior producer in the Chickasaw Nation's multimedia department, for his shared interest and lively conversations about Piominko. We owe a debt of thanks to the many museums, collections, and individuals that provided images and maps for the book. We are also grateful to the talented artist James Blackburn, who created sketches for it. We would be exceptionally remiss if we did not acknowledge the first-rate professionals at Chickasaw Press: Director Wiley Barnes, Suzanne Mackey, Corey Fetters, Hannah Waggoner, Marissa Moore, and Stan Nelson. In particular, Suzanne and Stan painstakingly eliminated repetitions, contradictions, and poorly worded sentences. The book is much more readable because of their fine editing skills.

Numerous family, colleagues, and friends also deserve recognition as well for their support. While each person merits a separate acknowledgment, space limitations prevent us from doing that. Please know, however, we haven't forgotten, and we remain grateful for the encouragement and assistance from each of you. With that said, we wanted to thank a few special individuals for their invaluable and immeasurable contributions to the creation of this story. Aside from Piominko, it is these individuals to whom we dedicate this book. I wish to thank my parents, John (who passed away near the completion of the book) and Myrna, who taught me the values that guide my life today. I also wish to thank my wife Vicki, and our children Cameron, Katie, and Kory, for reminding me of everything that is right in this world. Mitch wishes to especially thank John Ray and Lottye Betts Beasely for their friendship, support and shared love of Chickasaw history. He also wants to particularly thank his brother Steve for his advice and guidance. Lastly, our most important acknowledgment is to the accomplishments and memory of Piominko himself and his enduring legacy. Without him there would be no story that follows.

Thomas W. Cowger
Ada, Oklahoma
January 23, 2017

PIOMINKO

CHICKASAW LEADER

CHAPTER ONE

NEW EYESIGHT

———◦◦◦———

*"Nittak kanihmikma Naahollo micha Hattak Api' Homma' táwwa'at
ittinkana pisalikma, ishkin himitta' ishpisa' chihma'chi."*

*"Could I once see the day that whites and reds were all friends,
it would be like getting new eyesight."*

*~ Piominko to Governor William Blount and assembled leaders of the Chickasaw
and Choctaw Nations, Nashville conference grounds, August 8, 1792,
Chickasaw translation provided by John Dyson and Jerry Imotichey*

———◦◦◦———

BY the end of the eighteenth century, Piominko had witnessed many changes in the nearly fifty years that had passed since his birth. As he looked out
from his beloved Chokka' Falaa' (Long Town) village, which would one day
be the site of his final resting place, many thoughts must have raced through
his mind. From that vantage point, looking across the grassy plains scattered
with trees that stretched for a couple of miles, he could likely see the smoke
rising from the other nearby Chickasaw villages. Recently, he and his people
had successfully navigated some challenging and difficult times. While many
uncertainties remained, he had every right to feel a strong sense of pride at the
resiliency of his people and a renewed hope for an even brighter future.

Little could he have known that one day statues would be erected in his
honor, holidays and parks would bear his name, and cities would be proposed
in tribute to him. He likely didn't know that he represented one of the great

This bronze sculpture of Piominko by William Beckwith stands in front of the city hall in Tupelo, Mississippi. Commissioned by the Tupelo Rotary Club, it was unveiled during a public ceremony in 2005. *Photo by Corey Fetters*

minkos (leaders) of the Chickasaw Nation. During his lifetime his fame had spread as an orator, statesman, and diplomat. As an able leader, he skillfully protected and promoted Chickasaw sovereignty in the midst of vast changes occurring on the North American continent. His memory of President George Washington bestowing a peace medal on him for his significant contributions to the creation of the new American republic must have brought a smile to his face. He well understood that few Native American leaders could call President Washington a personal friend and be entertained at the President's House in Philadelphia. He would have also taken tremendous pride in knowing that the president viewed him as an invaluable ally and patriot to the new American cause, particularly when Piominko could have chosen instead to play all sides against each other. In the end, he decided that siding with the Americans also advanced the interest of his people, and from this path he never wavered. As he said in Nashville in 1792 to an assembled group of American and Chickasaw and Choctaw leaders, in his heart he longed for a day when "white and reds were friends." To him, no gift would be greater and that would be "like getting new eye-sight."[1] Unfortunately, he did not live long enough to see his hopes fulfilled. He did, however, witness the remarkable resiliency of his people in the face of difficult challenges. One can speculate that he would be exceptionally pleased by the continued vitality and strength of the "unconquered and unconquerable" Chickasaw Nation today.

While many of the details of Piominko's family background and his early years remain sketchy and elusive, some aspects of it can be fleshed out from available sources and stitched together to offer a somewhat more detailed account of his personal life. His story begins decades earlier with the birth of his mother in a small Chakchiuma (also spelled Chocchuma and sometimes referred to as the Saquechuma) village in present-day north-central Mississippi.[2] Little is known about either her or the Chakchiuma community she descended from. The available records remain silent on her name and family background.

The English translated the Chakchiuma name to mean "red crawfish," which also was the tribe's war emblem.[3] The Chakchiumas likely represent the merger of several closely affiliated groups that joined towns to form a

1. Governor Blount to the Head-men and other leaders of the Chickasaws and Choctaws, 8 August 1792, *American State Papers: Indian Affairs* 1: 287.

2. James R. Atkinson, *Splendid Land, Splendid People: The Chickasaw Indians to Removal* (Tuscaloosa: The University of Alabama Press, 2004), 126. Referencing Lyman Draper's interview with Malcolm McGee, Atkinson states that McGee said Piominko was a "Chickasaw-Chackchiuma mix."

3. Ibid., 16; James F. Barnett Jr., *Mississippi's American Indians* (Jackson: University of Mississippi Press, 2012), 78, 126.

Sketch of Piominko and President George Washington by James Blackburn

single polity.[4] While the exact number of tribal members in the early eighteenth century is unknown, one can get a rough idea of their numbers from several sources. Estimates suggest around sixty to seventy Chakchiuma families lived at this time at the confluence of the Yazoo and Yalobusha Rivers between Chickasaw and Choctaw territories.[5] Ethnographer, historian, and naturalist Antoine-Simon Le Page du Pratz stated in his travels through the area that there were not more than fifty Chakchiuma lodges. French explorer Jean-Baptiste Bénard de la Harpe observed around one hundred fifty members in his journeys through the region in 1722.[6] These numbers appear noticeably lower than a generation or two before. Several accounts suggest that in 1704 the French and their Native American allies destroyed nearly eighty percent of the Chakchiumas in retaliation for the murder of a missionary and three Frenchmen.[7]

While these early French sources help inform us of Chakchiuma tribal numbers and locations in the early eighteenth century, they also reveal something about Chakchiuma cultural characteristics. French explorer Pierre Le Moyne d'Iberville noted in his journals relating to his lower Mississippi valley explorations in the late seventeenth century that the Chakchiumas represented "a Chicacha nation."[8] His observations suggest that he thought they were related to the Chickasaws and speakers of the Muskogean language. Chickasaw and Choctaw origin stories also feature the Chakchiumas.[9] Caught between conflicting Chickasaw, Choctaw, and European interests, by the mid-eighteenth century the Chakchiumas had sustained significant population losses and had to frequently shift between varying alliances.

After years of Chakchiuma scalp and horse raids against them, Chickasaw warriors often sought retaliation against the Chakchiumas. It is known that a sizable Chickasaw, Natchez, and possibly Yazoo war party attacked a Chakchiuma village in 1732 and took women, and perhaps children, prisoners.[10] Smaller battles between the tribes continued for the next forty years, before coming to a head around 1770, when Chickasaw and Choctaw warriors launched a large attack that dealt a decisive blow to the Chakchiumas. Trapping the Chakchiumas in an area with few outlets for escape, the combined

---

4. Robbie Ethridge, *From Chicaza to Chickasaw* (Chapel Hill: The University of North Carolina Press, 2010), 77, 135.

5. Barnett, *Mississippi's American Indians*, 77.

6. Both Du Pratz and La Harpe's numbers are found in John R. Swanton, *Indian Tribes of the Lower Mississippi and Adjacent Coast of the Gulf of Mexico*, Bureau of American Ethnology, Bulletin 43, Smithsonian Institution (Washington DC: Government Printing Office, 1911), 294.

7. Ibid.

8. Pierre Iberville, *Iberville's Gulf Journals*, trans. and ed. Richebourg McWilliams (Tuscaloosa: University of Alabama Press, 1981), 175.

9. Barnett, *Mississippi's American Indians*, 78.

10. Atkinson, *Splendid Land, Splendid People*, 38.

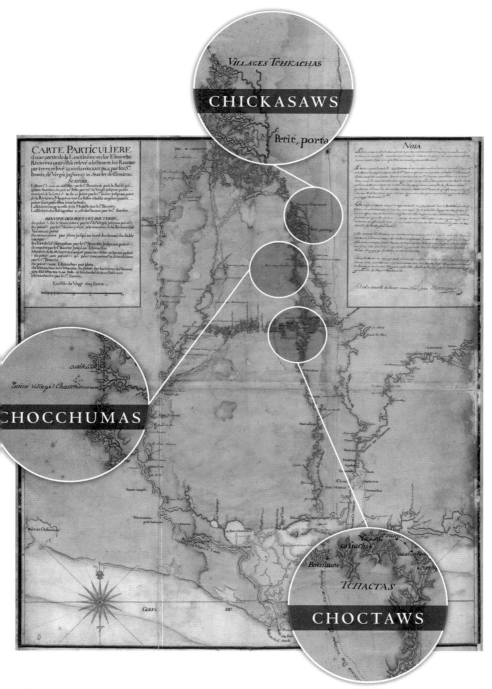

This enhanced 1743 French Demarigny map of the Mississippi River valley shows the close proximity of Piominko's mother's tribe, the Chakchiumas (Chocchumas), to the Chickasaws and Choctaws. *Mississippi River Valley Map, courtesy of Chickasaw Nation Archives*

forces virtually eliminated all Chakchiuma males of age. Their anger spilled over to every animal in the villages, as they were reported to have killed all those as well. Some of the women and children were spared and taken as captives. Eventually some of these prisoners of war were absorbed into the Chickasaw or Choctaw Nations, as the Chakchiumas effectively ceased to exist as a tribe following the attack.[11] Moreover, throughout the period, as the Chakchiumas came under attack from various tribes and their numbers continually decreased, some Chakchiuma members voluntarily sought refuge with their Chickasaw neighbors. In essence, Piominko's mother may fit either scenario, coming to the Chickasaws as a refugee or a spoil of war who was later adopted into the Nation. Regardless, it is likely in one of the Chickasaw villages that she met the Chickasaw warrior she eventually married. Unfortunately, her clan affiliation is not recorded or known to us today. The matrilineal clans of the Southeastern tribes played a critical role as they united them within a system of shared obligation and mutual respect. Clans determined family relationships, inheritance of property, duties and responsibilities, and often status. Sometimes clan affiliation cut across inter-tribal lines.

Piominko never knew his father, as he was killed by Shawnee warriors in skirmishes near the time of Piominko's birth. According to Edward Albright in his book, *Early History of Middle Tennessee*, Piominko's father was a prominent Chickasaw minko. Albright's account states that in 1788, while meeting with settlers at Bledsoe's Station near present-day Castilian Springs, Tennessee, Piominko mentioned his father's death and the continual need to expel the Shawnees from the Cumberland Valley. Not mincing words he told his ready listeners that the Shawnees had encroached on Chickasaw lands in the region.[12]

In the early 1700s a sizable number of Hathawekela Shawnees migrated into the Cumberland Valley. The Chickasaw Nation claimed the greater part of western Tennessee and with Cherokee assistance drove Shawnee Indians from the valley with several attacks between 1710 and 1715. By 1730 most Shawnees had fled north, but a handful remained. In 1745 another group of Shawnees attempted to resettle along the Cumberland River. Growing impatient with threats to their resources and territorial hunting lands, Chickasaw warriors immediately pushed back against the resettlement attempt. As they

---

11. Swanton, *Indian Tribes of the Lower Mississippi*, 295-296; Horatio Cushman, *History of the Choctaw, Chickasaw and Natchez* (Greenville, Texas: Headlight Printing House, 1899), 243-245.

12. Edward Albright, *Early History of Middle Tennessee* (Nashville, TN: Brandon Printing Company, 1909), 11. Piominko (or Albright) erroneously suggested the battle to drive the Shawnee out occurred in 1682. He is also reported to have said in 1788 that he was 106 years old. Neither were true, and it could be that the sources Albright used to reconstruct that part of the history were wrong. Piominko's account of his father's death near the time of his birth, however, would line up with the last skirmishes with the Shawnee and not the earlier ones.

did, many of the larger attacks on the Shawnees took place near present-day Nashville, Tennessee, and the most decisive battle occurred in 1745. Following this pivotal clash and numerous other Chickasaw raids on Shawnee parties over the next decade, Chickasaw warriors finally succeeded in permanently driving them out of the region in 1756.[13] It is in one of these campaigns that Piominko's father likely died. Like that of Piominko's mother, his name is lost to the written record.

Piominko's birth name is unknown, but it is known that he held several Chickasaw titles throughout his lifetime. Within Southeastern communities, titles and names for warriors and leaders changed frequently as they rose in status and with each new accomplishment. Piominko was no exception. He was often referred to by Euro-Americans as "Mountain Leader," and it appears probable that sometime early in his adult life he also went by the Chickasaw title "Tushatohoa." He signed the Virginia-Chickasaw Treaty of 1783 with the combined designation Tushatohoa the Mountain Leader. Linguist John Dyson speculates that the signature on that document could be an anglicized attempt by officials to write *Tashka Imalhtaha*, which in Chickasaw means "Consummate Warrior." However, Chickasaw anthropologist LaDonna Brown believes that Tushatohoa is probably correct.

Another uncertainty is whether his title of Piominko was that of a war leader or a peace leader. Brown explains that unfortunately Euro-Americans attempted to record the names phonetically in English and other languages as they heard them pronounced, without providing information about towns and clans with which they were affiliated.[14] Southeastern tribes often divided themselves and their clans into red and white moieties. Red moieties signified war and white represented peace. The failure to ensure the correct spellings and the absence of other cultural identifiers and insights makes it nearly impossible to know with certainty the meaning of many Chickasaw names.

Written primary sources of the period attempt to spell Piominko's name multiple ways, including Paimingo, Opiamingo, Opia Mingo, Pyo Mingo, Opoiaming, and Opaya Mingo or other similar combinations. In the eighteenth century, English speakers likely pronounced his name or war title as "Pie-yo Minko," reflecting a combination of the original Chickasaw words, *hopayi* (prophet) and *minko* (leader). Contemporaries of his generation would likely find today's frequently used, incorrect pronunciation of "Pee-oh-mingo" as unrecognizable to them.[15] Most of those contemporary sources, however,

---

13. Ronald N. Satz, *Tennessee's Indian Peoples: From White Contact to Removal, 1540-1840* (Knoxville: University of Tennessee Press, 1979).

14. LaDonna Brown, email message to Tom Cowger, November 2, 2015.

15. John Dyson, email message to Tom Cowger, March 22, 2016; John Dyson, *The Early Chickasaw Homeland: Origins, Boundaries and Society* (Ada, OK: Chickasaw Press, 2014), 65.

generally refer to him interchangeably as Mountain Leader and/or Piomingo, and these titles have been the most widely accepted until recently. Chickasaw scholars today suggest that the latter is in all likelihood a corrupted pronunciation form of the more correct Piominko. In 2014, the Chickasaw Nation adopted the latter spelling as the official one. On April 28, 2014, the tribe dedicated a statue in his likeness called *Hopayi' Minko'* on the grounds of the historic Chickasaw National Capitol in Tishomingo, Oklahoma, using the Chickasaw spelling of one of the titles his name may have represented. Other linguists maintain that the title may instead translate as "Principal War Oracle." Designated as a war prophet, the position holder could predict military outcomes and use appropriate measures to ensure the safety of the warriors under their charge.[16] Either way, his title appears to be one of great distinction, and he is simply referred to today by the Chickasaw Nation and others as Piominko. He has erroneously been linked to an earlier Chickasaw war minko named Opoia Mattaha (Paya Mattaha, or Hopayi' Imalhtaha', "Accomplished War Leader") who was also known as Piominko. Ethnohistorian James Atkinson notes in his book *Splendid Land, Splendid People* these were different Chickasaw leaders based on the discrepancy of their ages and the times they lived. Atkinson also notes that there were earlier references to several other Piominkos that were called Pia Mingo Euleuroy, Paye Mingo Belixy, or Paheminggo Elookse, and that these were also different individuals and not the Mountain Leader.[17]

Chickasaw interpreter Malcolm McGee provides several important clues relating to Piominko and his family. Having interacted with and lived among the Chickasaws since his childhood in the mid-1760s, McGee agreed in 1841, near the end of his life, to an interview with journalist and historian Lyman Draper near present-day Pontotoc, Mississippi. Draper conducted the interview with McGee near the home of Reverend Thomas C. Stuart, missionary and superintendent of the Presbyterian Monroe Mission school for Chickasaw students. Nearly destitute from dishonest associates and bad business deals, McGee found himself homeless late in his life. His friend Reverend Stuart helped him build a cabin where he lived many years near Stuart's property. In the winter of 1848, McGee's Chickasaw daughter traveled from Indian Territory to Mississippi and convinced him to return with her. He died nearly a year later on November 5, 1849, at the age of eighty-nine. He is buried in the Boggy Depot Cemetery near Atoka, Oklahoma.[18]

---

16. John Dyson, email message to Tom Cowger, November 25, 2015; John P. Dyson, "Chickasaw War Names and Four Homeland Colberts: William, George, Levi and Martin," *The Journal of Chickasaw History and Culture* 17, no. 2 (Fall 2015): 12-13.

17. Atkinson, *Splendid Land, Splendid People*, 125, 127.

18. T.C. Stuart to Unknown Recipient, 7 September 1861, in George Howe, *History of the Presbyterian Church of South Carolina, Vol. II* (Columbia, SC: W.J. Duffie, 1883), 442-444.

At the time of the interview with Draper, Piominko had been dead nearly forty years and McGee was in his eighties, but his mind remained remarkably clear about many of the critical Chickasaw events of the late eighteenth and early nineteenth century. Not only was McGee a contemporary of Piominko who interacted with him on a daily basis, but he was also married to a Chickasaw and familiar with Chickasaw culture and thus provides invaluable insights about Piominko. Despite some shortcomings in terms of offering a complete portrait of Piominko the person, McGee's narrative is undoubtedly the closest we will likely get to a critical, firsthand account.[19]

McGee offered several physical and intellectual descriptions of Piominko. According to McGee, he favored his mother and the Chakchiuma people in his complexion, which was much lighter than most Chickasaws of the time. He was short to average in height and of medium build. Additional sources verify this, including a wooden nautical figurehead probably created in his likeness while he posed for the sculptor who created it (as discussed in chapter 5). Scottish merchant and influential trader William Panton, in a somewhat less than flattering way, paid him a backhanded compliment when he characterized him as "a sensitive talkative little Indian." Favorably impressed by him, a Tennessee settler who knew him asserted he was "naturally one of the shrewdest of men ... a true and good man; and ... was among the smartest men by nature I ever saw. I have no doubt but if he had an education, he would have made a great statesman."[20] With or without a formal education, Piominko, by any measure, was a preeminent statesman and was highly respected by most who knew him.

Piominko was born around 1750 in Chokkilissa' (Old Town), a Chickasaw village in present-day Lee County, Mississippi, and he spent his earliest years there. Ironically, his final resting place in Long Town is a relatively short distance away. He spent several of his adolescent years with the Cherokees to the east. McGee suggested that when a Chickasaw individual killed his favorite brother, Piominko's mother moved them to a Cherokee village to help ease the loss. He remained there several years before returning to the Chickasaw Nation just prior to the Cherokee war with the British in roughly the mid-1770s.[21] Atkinson verifies and documents Piominko's years with the Cherokees. He writes:

Noted Cherokee chief Bloody Fellow stated in 1793 that

---

19. James R. Atkinson, "A Narrative Based on an Interview with Malcolm McGee by Lyman C. Draper," *Journal of Mississippi History* 66 (Spring 2004): 37-42.

20. The settler's direct quote and much of the additional insights in this paragraph come from Atkinson, *Splendid Land, Splendid People*, 126.

21. Atkinson, "A Narrative Based on an Interview with Malcolm McGee," 48-49; Atkinson, *Splendid Land, Splendid People*, 126.

Piomingo was his "old Friend & Can Speak my tongue as well as a Cherokee." Further confirmation of McGee's statement lies in the revelation by noted Cherokee chief Little Turkey in 1795 that Piomingo was his nephew and the latter had a son living in the Cherokee Nation.[22]

It appears from these and other statements that Piominko was well-liked and respected by his Cherokee hosts. During those adolescent years he was starting to acquire leadership skills that would later serve him well and propel him into leadership positions. Little Turkey rose to great prominence within the Cherokee Nation as a beloved man on the general council and later in 1794 as the first principal chief of the united Cherokee. He held this title until his death in 1801. In discussions in 1792 to settle boundaries between the Chickasaws, Cherokees, and Choctaws, Piominko also verified that Little Turkey was indeed his uncle.[23] Southeastern regional author Don Martini maintains that Piominko's mother had another son while living with the Cherokees whom she named Kaiateh.[24] Other documents show an individual by that name who later gained some minor Cherokee prominence and would have been the right age to be a contemporary of Piominko. If Martini is correct, and the two were half-brothers, it is possible that relationship later averted some conflicts between Chickasaw and Cherokee interests, as the two tribes were not always friendly toward each other. Since the father of Kaiateh is unknown, and Little Turkey was Piominko's uncle, it is logical to assume that after the death of her first husband, Piominko's mother married Little Turkey's brother. Another plausible explanation would be if Piominko and Little Turkey referred to themselves as culturally related through tribal or clan adoption, but not literally. The former and not the latter seems more likely. Since the Cherokees were often referred to as the Mountain Indians by others, it is likely that his association with them produced his later nickname of Mountain Leader.[25]

At some point Piominko married Molletulla (sometimes spelled Malataloya), which is likely an anglicized version of her actual name.[26] Little is known today about her or her tribal affiliation since it is possible he met her in a Cherokee village, but it appears she was Chickasaw. John Dyson suggests that her actual name may have been Malit Ola, which roughly translates in Chickasaw to "she runs away making chirping sounds." He said the alternative Chickasaw spelling of her name may represent Imolat Ala' and translates to "she made a

---

22. Quoted in Atkinson, *Splendid Land, Splendid People,* 126.

23. Governor Blount to the Head-men and Chiefs of the Chickasaws and Choctaws, 8 August 1792, American State Papers: Indian Affairs 1: 286.

24. Don Martini, *Who Was Who Among the Southern Indians a Genealogical Notebook, 1698-1907* (Falkner, MS: Pioneer Publishing Company, 1998), 532.

25. Atkinson, *Splendid Land, Splendid People,* 126.

26. Unknown author, "Piomingo," *Journal of Chickasaw History* 8, no.1, series 29 (2002): 4.

These ceremonial pottery vessels, known as cross-in-circle bowls, were found at the Chokkilissa' (Old Town) village site near Tupelo, Mississippi, in the 1950s. Their unique four-lobed shape is representative of the cross-in-circle motif, which was an important symbol in ancient Chickasaw culture, and they are thought to have been used in annual renewal rites such as the Green Corn ceremonial. Tempered with finely crushed fossil shell, they are typical of the type of Chickasaw pottery that Piominko, who was born at Chokkilissa', would have been familiar with. These vessels were donated to the Chickasaw Nation in 2013 and are now housed in the Holisso Research Center at the Chickasaw Cultural Center in Sulphur, Oklahoma. *Photo by Branden Hart*

Ceremonial cross-in-circle bowls, *photo by Branden Hart*

sound for her/them [mother/mother and midwives] when she was born," and "she literally uttered [something] for her/them as she arrived."[27] According to several accounts, she was tall, had long, beautiful braided hair, and dressed nicely. Non-native officials often paid her proper deference as the spouse of a noted leader by offering her a variety of gifts including clothes, ornaments, and on one occasion, a small hatchet.[28]

Piominko appears to have had several brothers, including those previously mentioned. While leading a unit up the Tennessee River on a diplomatic mission to the Chickasaw Nation in 1790, Major John Doughty noted that he met Piominko and another of his brothers named Alaitamoto. Dyson maintains that the correct spelling of the name is probably Holahta' Imalhtaha', and it means "Consummate Holahta." The latter represents an unknown, earned rank, and he apparently was quite successful at it. Piominko and his brother met Major Doughty in hopes of acquiring much-needed supplies. Little else is known about this brother. In the summer of 1789 a Creek war party killed Piominko's nephew and another of his brothers, Panss Fallayah (Ipashi' Falaa') or Long Hair. Apparently this brother also held some Chickasaw status and several years later Piominko sought justice and retribution for their death.[29] This incident will be discussed in greater detail in chapter 3, as it heightened tensions between the Creek and Chickasaw Nations.

Molletulla and Piominko had at least two children: a son and a daughter. Some sources suggest their son may have been called Mountain Leader Tippo, while other sources refer to their son as Butterboo.[30] Whether Mountain Leader Tippo and Butterboo are the same son or two different sons cannot be determined. On at least one occasion, Butterboo rescued a "white captive" from the Creeks. Ironically, at almost the same time, his father negotiated the release of a young man of Chickasaw/Creek descent who had recently been captured by a Southwest Territory militia.[31] Piominko apparently had a son living with the Cherokee Nation. In a letter from Little Turkey to Southwest Territory militia general James Robertson in 1795, the Cherokee leader wrote he hoped for peace with the newly created United States. In particular, he reminded him of the recent successful discussions they had in Knoxville. Little Turkey so valued those negotiations that he wanted his nephew, Piominko, to be apprised of the specific details and sent them to him by a carefully selected

27. John Dyson, email message to Tom Cowger, November 25, 2015.

28. A.W. Putman, *History of Middle Tennessee; Or, Life and Times of Gen. James Robertson* (Nashville, TN: Published for the Author, 1859), 524.

29. Atkinson, *Splendid Land, Splendid People,* 134, 144.

30. Atkinson, *Splendid Land, Splendid People,* 179.

31. Both Butterboo and the incidents are mentioned in W.W. Clayton, *History of Davidson County, Tennessee, with Illustrations and Biographical Sketches of its Prominent Men and Pioneers,* (Philadelphia, PA: J.W. Lewis & Co., 1880), 56.

Sketch of Piominko by James Blackburn

messenger. Calling the Chickasaws "his brothers," Little Turkey chose to send Piominko's son, who apparently was living in one of the Cherokee villages. He likely did this because it increased the probability that the message would get through, as Piominko's son would be given safe passage through Chickasaw lands. He also wanted Piominko to see his son and then send a response back with him to Little Turkey.[32] It stands to reason that if his son, or one of them, was a Cherokee messenger for his uncle Little Turkey, then it is quite possible that Molletulla was also Cherokee and Piominko met her during his time with the Cherokee Nation. Perhaps another explanation would be if Piominko had more than one wife, but there doesn't appear to be any evidence to support either of these conclusions.

In the 1930s, a local Mississippi author attempted to identify the location of the mountain where Piominko earned the name Mountain Leader, and where Little Turkey and perhaps Piominko's messenger son lived. E.T. Winston penned at least one local history book and served as the editor of a newspaper in Pontotoc, Mississippi, and his stories were widely read. He published a story in 1936 which was reprinted later that year in a centennial insert of *The Times Post*, published in neighboring Chickasaw County, Mississippi, in which he suggested that through sleuthing and deductive reasoning he had discovered the location of the mountain. He maintained that he had learned that the Chickasaw word *yanta* translated to "runner or messenger" and *ishali* translated to "main or superior." When the words are combined, he suggested, it is close to *yantaishahli*, (or *yantamain*, by blending Chickasaw with the English translation of the later part). Winston then attributed that as the name of Piominko's son who served as the Cherokee messenger. Winston then made a bold assertion that early non-Native settlers struggled to spell and pronounce the name *Yantamain* and inadvertently converted it into a phonetically similar sounding "Johnny Main." In the Skuna bottom region south of Pontotoc County in present-day Calhoun County, Mississippi, there is a hill that locals refer to as "Johnny Main's Mountain." Here, Winston says, is "Piomingo's Mountain" and the location where he spent his years with the Cherokees.[33] While it is an interesting and curious story, unfortunately there is little evidence to

---

32. Little Turkey to Gen. James Robertson, 10 April 1795 in "Correspondence of General James Robertson," *The American Historical Magazine* 4, no. 1 (January 1899): 191-192; Little Turkey to Wm. Blount, 10 April 1795, in "Correspondence of General James Robertson," *The American Historical Magazine* 4, no. 3 (July 1899): 249.

33. A copy of the 1936 reprinted article by E.T. Winston titled "Piomingo, the Mountain Leader" was provided by Jonathan D. Reeves of the Chickasaw County Historical Society in an email from Reeves to Mitch Caver, September 9, 2013. Unfortunately, the article did not provide information as to the date the article was published, the volume number, or the page it appeared. Aside from other newspaper accounts, Winston also published *Father Stuart and the Monroe Mission* (Meridan, MS: Press of Tell Farmer, 1927).

support Winston's claim and it is likely a fabrication or a stretched account at best. Dyson maintains there is no historical or linguistic proof for Winston's assertions. The Cherokee never lived in the Calhoun County area of Mississippi, Dyson argues, and there are no Chickasaw words that resemble the ones Winston used. Messenger in Chickasaw, he states, is *anompa shaali'* and not *yanta*.[34] Winston also erroneously refers to Piominko's uncle as Little Turtle, not Little Turkey. Winston's claim, however, offers an example of the difficulties one encounters in trying to separate known details of Piominko's early life from speculation.

It is known, however, that Piominko had a daughter, and she is mentioned in correspondence from various American officials. In a letter to President George Washington in late 1795, Piominko requested that the president consider educating his children, especially his daughter so she could learn how to read and write. Washington's secretary of war, Timothy Pickering, instructed General James Robertson that the president wished to honor Piominko's petition as long as the expense for doing it was reasonable. Pickering then directed Robertson to inform him of the costs of educating her and to meet any other moderate requests that Piominko may have for supplies.[35] This high-level correspondence exchange not only confirms he had a daughter, but also his hopes for her. Equally important, it demonstrates how much Washington and his cabinet members valued Piominko as a friend and ally.

Regrettably, we do not know for sure his daughter's name, but some genealogists speculate that she later married William Mizell (sometimes spelled Measels). In particular, these family historians maintain that she went by the name Mary Polly. They often point to the 1820 census and the September 7, 1809, will of William Mizell, where Mary and several children of the couple are mentioned. While the possibility exists, it remains difficult to verify that Mary and Piominko's daughter are the same person as conclusive evidence has not yet surfaced. It is known that Mizell served as both an interpreter and secretary for Piominko and later ran a trading post at Chickasaw Bluffs, Tennessee, near modern-day Memphis. Piominko thought highly enough of Mizell that in 1795 he requested General Robertson assign Mizell to serve as his personal interpreter.[36] Later, Mizell's son John also served as a Chickasaw interpreter, and his name appears as a witness on some treaty negotiations.

While little is known of Piominko's parents and ancestry, his childhood

---

34. John Dyson, email message to Tom Cowger, October 11, 2016. Dyson says that "Winston seems to have taken the Choctaw term 'i_shahli,' which is an auxiliary that serves as a comparative or superlative and gotten his 'main/superior' designation from that."

35. Gen. James Robertson to Unnamed Individual, 10 September 1795 in "Correspondence of General James Robertson," *The American Historical Magazine* 4, no. 1 (January 1899): 72-73.

36. Opiamingo to Gen. James Robertson, 1 September 1795, in "Correspondence of General James Robertson," *The American Historical Magazine* 4, no. 1 (January 1899): 68.

Memorial markers honoring the Chickasaws that lived at Chokka' Falaa' (Long Town). The markers are located on North Mississippi Medical Center property in Tupelo, near Longtown Medical Park. *Photo by Corey Fetters*

experiences, and his immediate family, they certainly shaped him. Clearly, he was favored with the skills and understanding necessary to meet the exceptionally difficult challenges of the times in which he lived. By the time he left the Cherokee village of his uncle Little Turkey as a young adult, he was coming of age and ready to fulfill his Chickasaw destiny. Returning home to his place of birth as a rising Chickasaw warrior, he began to passionately defend Chickasaw land and sovereign rights, earning the respect of those he dealt with. It was this passionate defense of his people and his skill as a diplomat which would eventually come to define his legacy.

CHAPTER TWO

BROTHERS NEVER FALL OUT

"My former Friends, we mean to Conclude A Peace With you. As Brothers Never falls out with Other, but they make Friends again If it is agreable to you, it is our Desire to be at Peace with you, that Our Corn may grow, and Our stocks Increase for the Bennifitt of our Child'r Hereafter."

– Piominko and three other Chickasaw leaders, July 9, 1782, in an open letter to American officers in forts throughout the Cumberland Valley

---

IN the decades prior to Piominko's birth, rapidly expanding European empires radically altered the cultural, political, economic, and social lives of the Southeastern Native societies they continued to encounter. The tumultuous times created both new opportunities and additional problems. By 1715 the Indian slave trade's vigorous thirty-year run was winding down. The trafficking of slaves had been driven by a flourishing Atlantic market that linked primarily Carolina-based English traders with various Indian communities, which were seen as sources of both potential slaves and slave catchers. The complicated trade network partnered merchants in Europe, West Africa, the Caribbean, and elsewhere in the Americas. Native participants in the slave trade prized the European goods that the selling of captured Indian slaves brought them, particularly guns and ammunition.[1]

In many ways participation in the trade meant survival, as a proactive response was better than a defensive one and the acquisition of guns strengthened one's hand. Native communities understood that for numerous reasons it was better to be the raiders than the raided. It also strengthened Chickasaw alliances with the English while some of their rivals partnered with the French. Unfortunately, the slave trade also dispersed and decimated significant numbers of Native populations in the Southeast. It strained relationships between neighboring tribes as it brought similar cultural groups, like the Chickasaws and Choctaws, into close competition with each other and forced them to choose sides with European powers, often at the expense of continued deteriorating relations. Scholars Robbie Ethridge and Sheri M. Shuck-Hall suggest that the disruption and instability that Europeans brought to the region essentially created a "shatter zone," as European-introduced systems splintered, stressed, and altered Native American communities and pressured them to seek ways to reestablish order in an ever-shifting landscape.[2] Those divides would only grow wider during Piominko's leadership as boundaries and alliances became of even greater importance.

As the Indian slave trade wound down, a lucrative and complex market in deerskins supplanted it. High European demand for deerskins and other furs dramatically transformed Indian communities into a labor-intensive business of hunting and tanning hides. In the process, it drew them even more heavily into mercantilism practices that offered valued trade goods in exchange for a currency set in fur. Prior to European contact, the same hides served utilitarian, ceremonial, and diplomatic purposes, and the exchange of deerskins between Southeastern tribes represented bonds of friendship.[3] After Europeans arrived, natives began to see deerskins and furs as a commodity, which greatly altered their view of their ecosystem and the roles of individuals within their communities. It also intensified hostilities between neighboring tribes and competing European interests all wanting to control the trade and the enormous profits from it. The high stakes led to increased warfare. In particular, throughout much of the period the French and allied Choctaw forces repeatedly attacked Chickasaw villages and strongholds, a situation which finally culminated around the start of the French and Indian War/Seven Years' War in 1754. Perilous and intricate relationships forged between Southeastern tribes

---

1. Alan Gallay, *The Indian Slave Trade* (New Haven: Yale Press, 2002), 311. Gallay's prizewinning book intricately details the dynamics and complexities of the slave trade.

2. Robbie Ethridge and Sheri M. Shuck-Hall, eds., *Mapping the Mississippian Shatter Zone: The Colonial Indian Slave Trade and Regional Instability in the American South* (Lincoln: University of Nebraska Press, 2009).

3. James Barnett Jr., *Mississippi Indians* (Jackson, MS: University Press of Mississippi, 2012), 108.

Sketch of a trade negotiation between a Chickasaw warrior and a European trader by James Blackburn

and colonial powers during the slave and deerskin trade periods dramatically and irrevocably transformed the region as expanding boundaries, new trading partners, and escalating warfare turned the area upside down.

The end of the Seven Years' War in 1763 slightly clarified the imperial struggle, as it left the Chickasaw Nation with two European powers to contend with: Spain and England. France had lost the war to England and largely vacated North America. The 1763 Treaty of Paris essentially divided French Louisiana between Spain and England. Spain received New Orleans and all lands west of the Mississippi River. England now possessed all lands east of the river. After the war, colonial traders flooded areas near Chickasaw villages hawking alcohol and trade items to encourage deerskin production. Newly passed parliamentary laws to slow and regulate that trade had little effect much to the chagrin of Chickasaw leaders. Growing numbers of Chickasaw mixed-bloods also exerted more influence in tribal affairs and significantly changed traditional political and social systems. In particular, the numerous sons of James Colbert were coming of age. Colbert, a trader who had lived in Chickasaw country since his youth and spoke the language fluently, married several Chickasaw wives. The male offspring of those unions went on to help shape many Chickasaw council decisions and other matters as their roles increased. Colbert and several of his children had profitable businesses and comfortable homes and some owned slaves.[4] Other grown children from families with English fathers such as the McGillivrays, Seeleys, Allens, Loves, Browns, Albertsons, Kemps, and Perrys also vied for larger tribal roles.[5] The generational and cultural changes brought by mixed-blood leaders sometimes put them at odds with full-bloods. In order to rise as a successful leader, Piominko needed the support of both mixed-bloods and full-bloods and he needed to bridge the gap between them.

Near the time Piominko reached manhood, he took initial steps to move center stage into the swift and ever changing world he inherited. At close to nineteen years of age, he led one of his first recorded war parties. Around the same time, in June of 1769, about twenty adventuresome colonial "long hunters" left Fort Chiswell, Virginia, in search of furs. Often gone from their homes for up to six months, the long hunters were noted explorers and hunters. The information they provided surveyors and various officials about the areas they trapped proved invaluable in the later settlement of Kentucky and Tennessee. Numerous geographic sites and place designations in both of these states today bear either the names of noted long hunters or monikers that the

---

4. Colin G. Calloway, *The American Revolution in Indian Country: Crisis and Diversity in Native American Communities* (Cambridge: Cambridge University Press, 1995), 221.

5. John P. Dyson, "Chickasaw War Names and Four Homeland Colberts: William, George, Levi, and Martin," *The Journal of Chickasaw History and Culture* 17, no. 2 (Fall 2015): 15.

explorers first coined.[6] While traveling through present-day middle and western Tennessee, the long hunters often cut through claimed Chickasaw boundaries. Those lands were often also contested Cherokee territory. Tired of the influx of trappers in their region, the Cherokees occasionally raided the exploration parties and took their pelts.[7]

The June 1769 long hunters' expedition left from Reed Creek, a tributary of the New River, in the southwestern corner of the Colony of Virginia. They passed through the Cumberland Gap and largely followed the Cumberland River as they made their way toward a destination somewhere near present-day Nashville, Tennessee. When they reached present-day northeastern Kentucky, they created a base camp along a creek and appropriately called it Station Camp Creek, which still bears that name today. They then split up in smaller parties that went in different directions, returning to the base camp periodically to drop-off the furs they harvested before leaving to hunt more. At one point while the camp was left unattended, a war party of around twenty-five Cherokees raided it taking about five hundred deerskins and some ammunition, clothing, and cooking utensils. When the trappers returned, they found the Cherokees had left them with little critical supplies.

While some of the group went in search of settlements to purchase goods to resupply themselves, others agreed to continue traveling south in search of furs. By April 6, 1770, more than half of the original long hunters, discouraged by their misfortune, decided to return home to the Colony of Virginia. The rest pressed on, heading south into present-day north-central Tennessee. The latter group included Uriah Stone, Kasper (sometimes spelled Gaspar) Mansker, John Baker, Thomas Gordon, Humphrey Hogan, Castleton Brooks, and four others. This remaining enterprising company of trappers built two boats and two canoes and commandeered another deserted boat they found as they traveled south on the Cumberland River. Loaded with newly hunted deerskins and fresh bear meat, they reached the site of an early French trading post named "French Lick" because it was a natural salt lick that attracted animals. Today the area is part of Nashville, Tennessee. In the eighteenth century, it was an area the Chickasaws considered to be part of their lands. Unbeknownst to the long hunters, Piominko and about twenty-five warriors happened to be crossing through the territory at nearly the same time the trappers arrived. The trappers' goods proved irresistible to Piominko and his party, who encountered the long hunters while in pursuit of a Seneca war party. They took several weapons and some ammunition, salt, and tobacco from

---

6. Emory L. Hamilton, "Historical Sketches of Southwest Virginia Publication 5: The Long Hunters," Historical Society of Southwest Virginia, (March 1970): 1.

7. Paul Bergeron, Stephen V. Ash, and Jeanette Keith, *Tennesseans and their History* (Knoxville, TN: University of Tennessee Press, 1999), 19-20.

the explorers, yet left them with the most valuable items: their lives and the deerskins. Eventually, the long hunters traded some furs to passing French boats, and nearly a year after they started their journey, they returned home. Today the area called Stones River in middle Tennessee, near Murfreesboro and south of Nashville, is named after long hunter Uriah Stone, memorializing those exploration efforts.[8]

Piominko had another important encounter early in his formative years as a warrior that had a fortuitous outcome, though it could have turned out far differently. In the early 1770s, Scottish-born Daniel Ross traveled from Baltimore to the northeastern corner of Tennessee as an orphaned youth. He then journeyed down the Tennessee River with others, on a flatboat he built himself, intending to start a trade business in the Cumberland Valley and Chickasaw lands. Taking advantage of the quicker method of passage, Piominko, who was traveling through the area, joined him onboard. As the boats wound their way below Lookout Mountain, near present-day Brown's Ferry and Chattanooga, obstructions in the river blocked their route forcing them ashore. When word quickly spread among the Chickamauga Cherokees (sometimes referred to as Chicomogie or Lower Cherokees) of the arrival of the outsiders near their villages, a crowd of Cherokees surrounded Ross, Piominko, and the others. Cherokee Chief Bloody Fellow recommended killing the group and seizing their goods. Instead, the uncertain Cherokee group consulted Scottish trader John McDonald, whom the Cherokees trusted and had traded with for years. McDonald persuaded them not to harm the group and encouraged Ross to open his trade store near Lookout Mountain, which he did. Years later Ross married McDonald's daughter Mollie, and they had a number of children together. Their third child, John Ross (Koo-wi-s-gu-wi), later rose to lead the Cherokee Nation through the difficult removal years.[9] In one of history's strangest twists, had the Bloody Fellow faction executed Ross, Piominko, and the others traveling by flatboat on that day, both the Cherokees and Chickasaws would have been robbed of two of their nations' most famous leaders, and the history of both communities would have been greatly altered. It is conceivable that Piominko's Cherokee background and language skills prevented their immediate death, allowing time for cooler heads to prevail. Piominko

---

8. Lyman Draper, "Life of Boone" (Unfinished Manuscript) Draper Manuscript Collection, 3 B 47-53, State Historical Society of Wisconsin; John Haywood, *The Civil and Political History of the State of Tennessee from its Earliest Settlement Up to the Year 1796, Including the Boundaries of the State* (Nashville, TN, Publishing house of the Methodist Episcopal church, South, 1891), 90-91.

9. Thomas McKenny and James Hall, "John Ross," in *History of the Indian tribes of North America: with Biographical Sketches and Anecdotes of the Principal Chiefs. Embellished with One Hundred Portraits from the Indian Gallery in the War Department at Washington, Vol. II*, (Philadelphia: D. Rice & Co., 1872), 159-160. This biography of John Ross can also be found online at Access Genealogy, https://www.accessgenealogy.com/native/john-ross-cherokee-chief.htm.

and Bloody Fellow crossed paths numerous times throughout the rest of their lifetimes. Later in his life, Bloody Fellow championed peace between Chickasaws and Creeks.

In 1771, around the same time as the Lookout Mountain event, Piominko traveled to Mobile with several other tribal members, including Paya Mattaha, whom the British considered a principal chief, and representatives from other Indian nations to meet with English officials. The southeastern colonial administrators often designated Mobile as a gathering site to let tribal representatives air their grievances and negotiate treaties in order to preserve critical alliances. In particular, much of the focus of this 1771-1772 conference centered around Indian complaints of unprincipled and corrupt traders.[10] Apparently feeling ill, Piominko left the discussions early to return to his village. He traveled in a caravan led by surveyor, artist, naturalist, and author Bernard Romans. Romans is credited with witnessing a bloodletting ceremony performed on Piominko on the return trip:

> (He) was this morning sick, on which occasion I saw one of his companions cut his temple with a flint, and, applying a cane about four inches long to the scarification, sucked it till he nearly filled it with blood, then threw it out, and repeated it several times; this is something like cupping; we were obliged to leave these two behind.[11]

Unfortunately, Piominko had little time to regain his strength following his illness on his return trip from Mobile before a sudden turn of events threatened to destabilize his region once again. The fruits of the Seven Years' War victory were short-lived for the English. Within a few years they were facing a colonial rebellion, and once again Indian nations were pressured to choose sides. Wisely, many Chickasaw leaders hoped to remain neutral in the Revolutionary War, which they largely saw as a struggle between English family members with whom they had often allied. The tense relationship between the mother country and its colonies confused and troubled tribal leaders who likely viewed the conflict as growing pains between a parent and an adolescent child who pushed for increased independence. Little could they, or the rest of the world for that matter, have foreseen the enormous global ramifications of the conflict.

At the onset of the war, Britain intended for the Chickasaw Nation to ally with them. In an open letter from British emissary Henry Stuart to settlers and Native American leaders in North Carolina and Virginia, the British offered

---

10. James R. Atkinson, *Splendid Land, Splendid People: The Chickasaw Indians to Removal* (Tuscaloosa: University of Alabama Press, 2004), 97-98.

11. James H. Malone, *The Chickasaw Nation: A Short Sketch of a Noble People* (Louisville, KY: John P. Morton Company, 1922), 336.

their communities total protection in exchange for participation in the king's army. They requested five hundred warriors from the Chickasaw Nation and similar numbers from other Indian nations willing to join them. In addition to protection, the British promised a decisive and well-coordinated attack on the rebellious colonists and a victory that would allow them and their allies to control the Mississippi valley and Eastern Seaboard. Stuart offered market value for Chickasaw horses, pigs, flour, and other needed resources to supply the British army.[12] They also wanted Chickasaw warriors to serve as sentinels along the Mississippi, Tennessee, and Ohio Rivers and keep Continentals out of the lower Mississippi valley and Gulf Coast region. The Chickasaws refused and remained more interested in protecting their own interests than those of their former ally. Even efforts by James Colbert produced minimal results in recruiting warriors to patrol the pivotal waterways.[13]

American revolutionaries' attempts to persuade the Chickasaws to join their cause yielded similarly dismal results. Virginian messages sent to Chickasaw leaders attempting to persuade them to forge an alliance with them or face hostilities if they refused, failed to sway them from their carefully calculated nonpartisan stance. Certainly it was not in their best interest early in the war to choose sides, and they hoped England and its disgruntled rebel colonists would soon resolve their differences. By 1780, however, American insurgents tipped the delicate balance of Chickasaw desired neutrality with a strategy that threatened Chickasaw security and sovereignty. As early as 1777, Virginia Governor Patrick Henry had recommended construction of an American outpost or fort at the confluence of the Mississippi and Ohio Rivers. Ideally located, the proposed fort would afford Americans a base to protect their interests from the British and Spanish and to control access to both rivers. Henry maintained that building an outpost near the mouth of the Ohio would reduce the weapons flow from Britain to its Indian allies, including the Chickasaws. It would also further validate Virginia's attempts to extend land claims from the Eastern Seaboard into lands vacated by the French.[14]

Finding Henry's arguments reasonable, his successor as governor of Virginia, Thomas Jefferson, opted in 1780 to explore the construction of a fort in the recommended location. American Brigadier General George Rogers Clark then built Fort Jefferson on the high ground overlooking present-day Wick-

---

12. Letter from Henry Stuart to the Frontier Inhabitants of North Carolina and Virginia, 19 May 1776, American Archives: Documents of the American Revolutionary Period, 1774-1776, Northern Illinois Libraries, Digital Collections and Collaborative Projects, fourth series, vol. 6, part II, subpart 16-20, title no. 11, http://amarch.lib.niu.edu.

13. Calloway, *The American Revolution in Indian Country*, 222-227.

14. William W. Henry, *Patrick Henry: Life, Correspondence and Speeches, Vol. 1* (New York City: Burt Franklin, 1891), cxxii; William Hayden English, *Conquest of Country Northwest of River Ohio, 1778-1783* (Indianapolis: Bowen-Merrill, 1897), 666-667.

liffe, Kentucky. Clark incentivized civilian settlement at the fort with gener-
ous land warrants.[15] Developers of the site planned, appropriately, to name the
civilian community adjacent to the fort Clarksville. Clark's energetic attempts
to build the fort ran contrary to the recommendation of Jefferson, who had
instructed him to buy the land first.[16] Correspondence between Jefferson and
Clark at the time also reveals that both incorrectly assumed that the Cherokees claimed the land in question, a mistake that can be attributed to a lack of
understanding outsiders often had regarding the nature of tribal boundaries.
Though the Chickasaw Nation sometimes allowed other tribes permission to
hunt in their boundaries and the area of the fort was far removed from the core
of the Chickasaw villages in present-day northern Mississippi, it still represented the northwestern boundary of the Chickasaw Homeland. Had Jefferson and
Clark known the site was Chickasaw land, it would have made little sense to
build the fort there, provoking the Chickasaws and deliberately drawing them
into the war while American forces were already stretched thin fighting other
campaigns elsewhere.

The unwelcomed and uninvited intrusion by Clark and others brought
a swift response from Chickasaw warriors. When Clark finished construction of the fort and town and several hundred soldiers and settlers occupied
it, Chickasaw warriors immediately attacked it several times in small reconnaissance missions. In April of 1780, James Colbert led a large assault on the
fort. Piominko almost certainly participated in the attack.[17] Colbert's forces
successfully forced the settlers and soldiers to take refuge in the fort, burning
their houses as they sought shelter from the attack and killing or capturing
some of the fort's inhabitants. They then held the fort under siege for nearly a
year. Cut off from reinforcements and provisions and isolated on the edge of
the western frontier, the inhabitants had little hope to defend themselves or
the fort from the well-orchestrated blockade. The surviving occupants finally
evacuated the fort and settlement and abandoned any further hopes of creating
a post in Chickasaw territory. In effect, the Chickasaw victory immediately
brought an end to American efforts to control the lower Mississippi valley and
routes to threaten British West Florida.[18] While some perceived the attack on
Fort Jefferson as Chickasaw warriors aiding the British, in reality they were
protecting their homelands and controlling their own destiny. Once Clark and

---

15. James Alton James, ed., *Virginia Series Volume III: George Rogers Clark Papers, 1771-1781, Vol.
I*, (Springfield, IL: Trustees of the Illinois State Historical Library, 1912), 386-391.
16. Thomas Jefferson to Joseph Martin, 24 January 1780, *Virginia Series Volume III: George Rogers Clark Papers, 1771-1781, Vol. I* ed. James Alton James (Springfield, IL: Trustees of the Illinois
State Historical Library, 1912), 385-386.
17. James R. Atkinson, "A Narrative Based on an Interview with Malcolm McGee by Lyman
C. Draper," *Journal of Mississippi History* 66 (Spring 2004): 45.
18. Calloway, *The American Revolution in Indian Country*, 108.

In 1780 Thomas Jefferson, who was then governor of Virginia, requested American Brigadier General George Rogers Clark build a fort in Chickasaw territory near Wickliffe,
Kentucky. Building the fort without Chickasaw consent caused a rare conflict between
the Americans and the Chickasaws. *Portrait of Thomas Jefferson by Ken Corbett after
Rembrant Peale*

Jefferson constructed the fort and settlement without Chickasaw permission, they forced the Chickasaws' hand, and the Chickasaws quickly responded to protect their sovereign interests. While the British benefited from the fort's fall, they appear to have had little to do with orchestrating the attack. Colbert, Piominko, and the others who participated did so to preserve Chickasaw sovereignty and land. Two years after the fall of the fort, and perhaps seeking improved relations with the Americans, Piominko and three other Chickasaw leaders penned a letter justifying the attacks on Fort Jefferson. In the end, it boiled down to a simple explanation: "you Settled A Fort in Our Hunting ground without Our Leave And at that place you Suffered Most from Us."[19] The letter further explained their willingness to start anew, make peace, and attempt to settle past differences, rather than allowing those to divide them.

Nearly forty years after the controversy surrounding the construction and later abandonment of the fort, Jefferson, in a letter to Archibald Stuart, lawyer, politician, and father of Confederate General Jeb Stuart, recalled the events and his actions differently than his earlier correspondence and actions and other documents at the time suggest. Jefferson argued that Patrick Henry, as governor, unsuccessfully attempted to influence Piominko to part with the land. Not terribly surprised by the failure to acquire it, Jefferson said that "it [had] been a principle with the Chickasaws never to part with a foot of land." When he succeeded Henry as governor, Jefferson stated that his vigorous overtures to obtain the land failed, and he then instructed Clark to build the fort anyway. He maintained that it was intended to be a temporary structure until the war ended, and at that time the land would be "sacredly restored" to the Chickasaw Nation. Having conveyed and communicated that information to Chickasaw leaders, he wrongly expected no opposition or backlash against the fort's construction. Ironically, he recalled that Cherokee and Choctaw forces attacked it first at different times, before the final Chickasaw siege. The evidence does not support the previously mentioned tribes' involvement in attacks on the fort, and these were clearly Chickasaw assaults. He closed his letter by saying that as the new secretary of state under President George Washington he unsuccessfully tried to purchase the land for Virginia, though it was eventually acquired through later land treaties.[20]

Perhaps Jefferson's recollections of the incident became clouded with the passage of time, but there may be other explanations. It is equally possible that he was trying to distance himself from any responsibility for the situation

---

19. Message from the Chickasaw, July 9, 1782, in *Calendar of Virginia State Papers and Other Manuscripts from January 1, 1782, to December 31, 1784, Preserved in the Capitol at Richmond, Vol. III*, ed. Wm. P. Palmer (Richmond, 1883), 278.

20. Letter from Thomas Jefferson to Archibald Stuart, 15 March 1819, Jefferson Papers, Founders Online, National Archives.

by claiming they tried in good faith to purchase the land. When those efforts failed, they communicated their intent to use the land temporarily and return it. Therefore, he erroneously thought both parties were in agreement, and he didn't anticipate the conflict. Predictably, Chickasaw anger over the construction of the fort likely delayed initial American overtures to join their cause until much later, and Jefferson could have averted the unfortunate affair.

Colbert, who helped direct the attack on the fort, remained a staunch British loyalist throughout the war, as did several other Chickasaws. Recognizing his value, England commissioned Colbert as a captain "in His Majesty's service" in 1780.[21] The American Continental Army's alliance with France also often pushed Chickasaws to side with the English. Previous conflicts with France and a working relationship with the British made the difficult choice easier. Colbert's military band consisted of his sons and nephews, slaves, some Chickasaw warriors, British loyalists, and others who supported his goals and the goals of those with similar larger Chickasaw interests. Wounded in the siege of the fort, Colbert survived and he and his military unit continued other attacks. They patrolled the Mississippi River, striking and capturing ships, including some Spanish vessels after Spain entered the war in 1779. Colbert led a final attack in 1783 on a Spanish fort at Arkansas Post near present-day Pine Bluff, Arkansas. His military unit had grown to eighty-two members. With the Revolutionary War drawing to an end, the raid accomplished little. While Piominko had supported Colbert before, he doesn't appear to have participated in the later actions as other pressing concerns to protect Chickasaw interests occupied his attention.[22]

In January 1781, Piominko led an attack on a new American settlement to protect Chickasaw land interests near the Cumberland River and present-day Nashville. Piominko did not know at the time that the chance encounter with James Robertson, one of the leaders of that settlement, would change the course of American and Chickasaw history. The eventual intersection of the two men's paths began years before with risky land explorations and a disputed treaty. After several days of negotiations, led by land speculator Richard Henderson of North Carolina, Cherokee leaders Oconostota, Attakullakulla, and Savanukah agreed in mid-March 1775 to cede Cherokee land in exchange for a relatively small amount of valued goods. Representing nearly thirty thousand square miles, the resulting Sycamore Shoals Treaty of 1775, or Transylvania Land Purchase, included the land between the Ohio and Cumberland Rivers. Shortly after the ink had dried, the Cherokees maintained that Henderson and his party had deceived them and forged Oconostota's signature. Moreover,

---

21. Atkinson, *Splendid Land, Splendid People*, 105.
22. Kristofer Ray, ed., *Before the Volunteer State: New Thoughts on Early Tennessee, 1540-1800* (Knoxville: University of Tennessee Press, 2014), 146-47.

the Cherokee signatories had no authority to sell all the disputed land as the Chickasaws and Creeks also asserted claims to parts of it. Attakullakulla's son, noted Cherokee war chief Dragging Canoe, sought revenge and attacked settlers moving into the contested area.[23]

The prospects of available land proved too tempting for adventuresome frontier persons who risked Native American war parties and other hardships to set up communities. Henderson supported land speculators John Donelson and James Robertson to lead settlers into the Cumberland River region. Later called the "Father of Middle Tennessee," Robertson was a relatively tall and imposing figure with a gentle, calm, and unruffled demeanor. He and his wife had thirteen children, two of whom died in infancy. Tired of the autocratic rule of the royal North Carolina governor, William Tryon, Robertson explored the land west of the Appalachian Mountains as early as 1769 in an effort to relocate outside the reach of colonial administrators. On his first trip, Robertson, traveling alone, had crossed the mountains to the Holston and Watauga Rivers and on the return trip became lost and wandered for two weeks, nearly perishing before hunters helped him find his way home.[24] Despite his frustration with Governor Tryon, Robertson remained loyal to North Carolina.

Pleased, however, with the sites he saw as he explored the region in 1769, he and several like-minded North Carolinians, likely led by Daniel Boone, moved and settled three years later along a rocky stretch of Watauga River rapids in present-day Elizabethton, Tennessee. Known as the "Old Field," the Cherokee laid claim to the land. Needing protection, the settlers quickly built a fort on a knoll and elected Robertson its commander. He and his fellow pioneers then established the Watauga Association, which represented one of the first semi-autonomous constitutional governments west of the Appalachians. While they still likely considered themselves British subjects, the settlers elected Robertson and four others as magistrates for the new association.[25]

When word reached Robertson of Henderson's treaty at Sycamore Shoals, he made plans to relocate his settlement, along with others who wished to join him. Robertson appears to have known little of the discrepancies surrounding the treaty, and throughout his years on the frontier he consistently reached out to various Native American groups, eventually serving as an Indian agent for the federal government. Henderson sought a coordinated emigration between Donelson and Robertson. Robertson escorted an overland party nearly three hundred miles, while Donelson led another group of about thirty families by boat and planned to rendezvous with Robertson's overland group.

23. Calloway, *American Revolution in Indian Country*, 189-190.
24. A.W. Putnam, *History of Middle Tennessee: Or, Life and Times of General James Robertson* (Nashville, TN: Tennessee Historical Society, 1859), 20-21, 23.
25. Ibid., 28-30, 49-53.

Considered to be one of the "Fathers of Tennessee," James Robertson was an explorer, military leader, and Indian agent to the Chickasaws. He developed a lifelong friendship with Piominko, and with Piominko's assistance was able to lay the foundations of early Nashville and the state of Tennessee. *By Washington B. Cooper, circa 1840's*

Donelson's fleet, consisting of a variety of boats, navigated the Holston, Tennessee, Ohio, and Cumberland Rivers. The flotilla carried a sizeable number of elderly, women, children, slaves, and necessary settlement supplies. The party included Donelson's large family and Robertson's wife, Charlotte, and five of their children. Donelson's youngest daughter, Rachel, later married Andrew Jackson, the architect of Indian Removal. Robertson's overland group of nearly two hundred individuals included his brothers, Mark and John, as well as his eleven-year-old son, who tended and drove the livestock.[26]

Upon reaching French Lick in the blistering cold by Christmas Day 1779, Robertson's land group decided to settle there rather than continue upriver. The Donelson party united with them in April 1780, and together both groups cleared the land and built a community near the center of present-day downtown Nashville, Tennessee. The settlement included a one-acre stockade in an area that today is located in River Park just off First Avenue North in downtown Nashville. Donelson and Robertson planned to name it Nashborough in honor of Revolutionary General Francis Nash with whom Robertson served in the war. Instead, the settlers called it Bluff Station, since it stood on a rise that overlooked the river. Ideally located on the northern terminus of what would eventually come to be called the Mountain Leader's Trace and later the Natchez Trace, Robertson encouraged others to join the site. The settlers unanimously elected Robertson as the colonel over their militia and as their appointed leader. They immediately drew up a compact of government.[27] Chickamauga Cherokees repeatedly challenged the settlers' claims to the land. Led by Chickamauga Cherokee War Chief Dragging Canoe, warriors attacked the settlement at every opportunity. Other tribal groups also struck it multiple times, intent on driving the intruders out. Applying unrelenting pressure, they often destroyed the settlers' crops and livestock, killed individuals caught outside the stockade, and left the survivors with depleted food supplies and short on ammunition. In later attacks, Robertson lost two brothers and two sons. He escaped death twice and was wounded in more than one ambush.[28]

Robertson and the other settlers quickly built eight fortified "stations" named after members of the company.[29] Unfortunately, they created the stations on the south side of the Cumberland River on land not included by the Cherokees in their cession at Sycamore Shoals. Many of the regional tribes reluctantly shared part of the Cumberland Valley as hunting grounds and tol-

---

26. Ibid., 42-43; Bill Bays, *James Robertson, Father of Tennessee and Founder of Nashville* (Bloomington, IN: WestBow Press, 2013), 133.

27. Putnam, *History of Middle Tennessee*, 47-50, 55, 68.

28. Ibid., 72-83; Terry Weeks, "James Robertson," in *Tennessee Encyclopedia of History and Culture*, University of Tennessee Press, January 2010, https://tennesseeencyclopedia.net/entry .php?rec=1137.

29. Putnam, *History of Middle Tennessee*, 89.

erated occasional long hunters who passed through it, but the sight of forts with stockades, cabins, and families alarmed them. Piominko immediately recognized the stations as an unwelcome intrusion on Chickasaw lands. Robertson and the settlers named one of these enclosed forts with several cabins Freeland Station after brothers George, Jacob, and James Freeland, who helped settle the area. Built near a large sulphur spring, a few bison paths running through dense strands of cane connected the station to the recently created Bluff Station.[30]

On the evening of January 11, 1781, Robertson returned to the new settlement following an extended trip to Kentucky to purchase supplies, including ammunition. When he arrived at Freeland Station, where his family was staying, he learned his wife had recently given birth to a son. Exhausted, excited, and relieved, he stayed up late that evening while everyone else slept. Around midnight, Piominko and a party of nearly one hundred fifty warriors attacked the station. When the warriors inadvertently rattled the gate bar trying to gain entry into the post, Robertson immediately arose, grabbed his rifle, and yelled, "Indians! Indians!" The nearly dozen men in the stockade immediately rushed to the gate to defend it. Piominko's party entered the gate and killed one of the settlers and one of Robertson's slaves. The loud exchange of gunfire inside the station awoke the settlers at Eaton's Station and Fort Bluff. Robertson's militia at Fort Bluff fired a cannon in the direction of Freeland. Realizing that the other stations were likely to come to the assistance of the settlers under siege at Freeland, Piominko and his band withdrew to safety. In their retreat, one of Robertson's shots hit its mark and killed a warrior, and his fellow defenders wounded others. In addition to the two settlers killed at the start of the assault, the attackers burned a large supply of corn and destroyed much of the station's livestock and its fodder.[31]

Piominko's late-night attack forced Robertson and the others to abandon Freeland Station the next day. They withdrew to Fort Bluff and the security of the militia there. Of the original eight stations in the Cumberland Compact, only a few remained as Native American attacks, and the constant threat of them, took a toll. Most of the surviving Cumberland Valley settlers lost hope and bolted to Kentucky or to their former homes in the east. Dragging Canoe and his Chickamauga Cherokees struck some of the remnants who remained at Fort Bluff on April 2, 1781. He artfully drew Robertson's men outside the stockade and then blocked their retreat route back to the post. Robertson's wife cracked the fort gate slightly and unleashed the fort's dogs on the Cherokee assailants. The ensuing confusion allowed the trapped settlers to scurry

---

30. Ibid., 84.
31. Ibid., 123-125; Edward Albright, *Early History of Middle Tennessee* (Nashville, TN: Brandon Printing Company, 1909), 90-94.

back inside the safety of the fort. The Cherokees retreated with the settler's captured horses. Robertson and his family and other hardy pioneers decided to stick it out despite the Cherokee raid. While they endured difficulties sustaining themselves, the attacks started to diminish. A year later they moved back to Freeland Station.[32]

Word spread to Piominko and other Chickasaw leaders in late fall of 1781 that their frequent ally the British had surrendered to the revolutionary colonists. That unexpected turn of events at Yorktown, Virginia, forced Piominko to chart a new course. He could no longer afford to straddle a line of neutrality and found himself in an unenviable position. Anxious tribal groups in the Old Northwest threatened war to acquire new land near the Cumberland settlements, recently appointed American officials demanded alliances, Virginia sought land cessions, and Spain incited the tribes surrounding the Chickasaw Homeland to sign agreements in order to strengthen Spanish claims to the southeast. Within months, Chickasaw leaders astutely made peace overtures with the Americans.[33] Unsure of whom to negotiate with in the American transitional government, they used various intermediaries to reach out to the officials they perceived to hold authority over the Cumberland region, since the French Lick settlement laid within Chickasaw boundaries. Almost simultaneously, American representatives recognized the importance of making conciliatory peace gestures to the Chickasaw Nation. In April 1782, a Cherokee delegation visiting Colonel Evan Shelby at Beaver Creek along the Holston River delivered a message a Chickasaw courier had brought them. The courier wanted the Cherokees to help ensure the dispatch seeking peace was delivered to colonial Indian agent General Joseph Martin living in Virginia.[34]

When the Chickasaws didn't receive a reply from Martin, they penned another note on July 9, 1782, to George Rogers Clark, a noted Virginia militia officer who led several Revolutionary War campaigns in the Old Northwest.[35] Chickasaw headmen Minko Houma (Minko' Homma', "Red Leader"), Paya Mattaha, Tuskau Pautaupau (Tashka Patalhpo'), and Piominko addressed their second message not only to Clark but to all "the Commanders of Every Different Station between this nation and the Falls on the Ohio River." In their olive

---

32. Putnam, *History of Middle Tennessee*, 129-134, 139-143.

33. Ronald N. Satz, *Tennessee's Indian Peoples: From White Contact to Removal, 1540-1840* (Knoxville: University of Tennessee Press, 1979), 49.

34. Message from the Chief of the Chikasas, as delivered by the messenger to the Cherokees, 20 May 1782, in *Calendar of Virginia State Papers and Other Manuscripts from January 1, 1782, to December 31, 1784, Preserved in the Capitol at Richmond, Vol. III*, ed. Wm. P. Palmer (Richmond, 1883), 172-173.

35. Robert S. Cotterill, "The Virginia-Chickasaw Treaty of 1783," *The Journal of Southern History* 8, no. 4 (1942): 486.

branch to American officials they said:

> My former Friends, we mean to Conclude A Peace With you. As Brothers Never falls out with Other, but they make Friends again If it is agreable to you, it is our Desire to be at Peace with you, that Our Corn may grow, and Our stocks Increase for the Bennifitt of our Child'r Hereafter.[36]

Within two years following the letter both Minko Houma and Paya Mattaha died, leaving Piominko the most influential Chickasaw leader.

The signatories of the letter charged two Chickasaw warriors and Simon Burney with its delivery. Burney, who was an Englishman living in the Chickasaw Homeland, or one of Colbert's sons likely wrote the letter on behalf of the four Chickasaw leaders.[37] Burney and the two warriors left from Chickasaw villages bound for Kentucky in search of Clark. The important letter they carried allowed them to safely and easily pass through each American post on their route.

After a brief stop at French Lick, they arrived in Lincoln County, Kentucky, nearly a month after the Chickasaw leaders wrote the letter. Arriving under a peace banner, the Chickasaw party delivered the message to Colonel Benjamin Logan, the county lieutenant. Logan shared the message with Colonel John Bowman and John Donelson, one of the previously mentioned founders of the Cumberland settlements.[38] The letter noted that previous attacks on American settlements resulted from a defense of Chickasaw lands and not deliberate acts of war.[39] Upon receiving the note, Logan, Bowman, and Donelson immediately urged Virginia Governor Benjamin Harrison to establish a committee to meet with the Chickasaw leaders. Bowman and Donelson recommended convening at French Lick near the Cumberland stations. Robertson initially opposed the location of the planned meeting, fearing that it would endanger the settlers, but later agreed to the site. Perhaps he was also uncomfortable with the idea that Virginia proposed the negotiations and not North Carolina.[40]

Clark took the lead in laying the foundation with the Chickasaws for the planned meeting. He dispatched Captain Robert George and John Donne, who both served Clark in his Illinois Regiment of Virginia, to the heart of Chickasaw country in the fall of 1782. George and Donne presented the Chickasaws with Clark and Harrison's wish for peace and promises of future trade and

---

36. Message from the Chickasaw, July 9, 1782, in *Calendar of Virginia State Papers, Vol. III*, 278.

37. Atkinson, *Splendid Land, Splendid People*, 120; Calloway, *The American Revolution in Indian Country*, 231.

38. Cotterill, "The Virginia-Chickasaw Treaty of 1783," 486.

39. John Donelson to Gov. Harrison, 1 September 1782, in *Calendar of Virginia State Papers, Vol. III*, 284; Cotterill, "The Virginia-Chickasaw Treaty of 1783," 486.

40. John Reid to Gov. Harrison, 23 February 1784, in *Calendar of Virginia State Papers, Vol. III*, 562-564.

supplies. They did not raise other proposals intended to persuade Chickasaw officials to cede Kentucky lands after finding Chickasaw leaders adamantly opposed to new land negotiations.[41] Hoping to start their relationship anew and to put previous disagreements behind them, Piominko, Minko Houma, Paya Mattaha, and others responded to the call for peace and shifted the blame for previous misunderstandings to England:

> The English put the Bloody Tomahawk into our hands, telling us that we should have no Goods if we did not Exert ourselves to the point of Resentment against you, but now we find our mistake and Distresses. The English have done their utmost and left us in our adversity. We find them full of Deceit and Dissimulation and our women & children are crying out for peace.[42]

While they had clearly left their frequent British allies out to dry, Piominko and the others knew that diplomacy represented the only hope for a shared future as they then extended a hand of goodwill:

> Brothers let us light the old Council Fire and Smok together. let us bury the bones our slain on both sides and forgett all. let us think on the old Friendship that ware formerly Between us the Americans our Brothers. Let the Roads and water courses be open clear and sincear friendship be planted.[43]

When George and Donne failed to reach an agreement in October, Clark dispatched Major John Reid the next spring, in April 1783, to visit the Chickasaw villages and try once again. After several stops and delays, Reid, who had also served under Clark during the Revolutionary War, finally arrived at the Chickasaw villages in present-day northern Mississippi on July 28, 1783. Two guides and a member of the French Lick community led Reid to the villages. Chickasaw leadership then convened a tribal council at Chokkilissa' days later to discuss Reid's pitch for a peace agreement, which a British officer interpreted on behalf of Reid. After concluding that a path towards peace represented the best option, Piominko and the other Chickasaw leaders agreed to meet in French Lick during a full moon in October to conduct a treaty. Reid then invited the Delawares living along the Tennessee River, the Creeks, and the Choctaws to the proposed treaty gathering.[44]

---

41. Calloway, *The American Revolution in Indian Country*, 232.

42. Answer from Piamthihaw, Minohamah, Piamingo, Chambeau, the Red King and Several other Sachams and Warriors, 24 October 1782, in *Calendar of Virginia State Papers, Vol. III*, 357-358.

43. Ibid., 357.

44. Cotterill, "Virginia-Chickasaw Treaty of 1783," 493-494, 494n31.

By the time Reid departed their villages, Piominko and the other leaders had authored a letter to the Confederation Congress and the new president, which they wanted Reid to deliver to Clark. In the letter they expressed the predicament in which they found themselves: caught in a crossfire between Spain, the newly created United States, the self-interests of the states that made up the new republic, and the Illinois tribe threatening them. Without Britain's aid and support the Chickasaws didn't know where to turn. With a desire for the American leaders to "open your Ears to haer, and your heart to understand us," they were receptive to negotiations. Suggesting that Spain had offered them supplies and weapons in exchange for allying with them, the leaders insisted they preferred instead a partnership with the victorious colonists. In return they wanted land encroachments to stop, new trade agreements, protection, and reassurances of future harmony to satisfy the young, restless warriors who entertained offers from all parties.[45] Food shortages and a smallpox epidemic placed additional pressures on them to keep their nation united in uncertain times.[46] Confused by the political structure of the new American government and wondering who was in charge of it, they sought an open dialogue, sovereignty, and to be treated as equals:

> We Know not who to mind or who to neglect. We are told that the Americans have 13 Councils Compos'd of Chiefs and Warriors. We Know not which of them we are to Listen to, or if we are to hear some, and Reject others, we are at a loss to Distinguish those we are to hear. We are told that you are the head Chief of the Grand Council, which is above these 13 Councils: if so why have we not had Talks from you, – We are head men and Chiefs and Warriors also: and have always been accustomed to speak with great Chiefs & warriors – We are Likewise told that you and the Great men of your Council are Very Wise – we are glad to hear it, being assured that you will not do us any Wrong, and therefore we wish to Speak with you and your Council, or if you Do not approve of our so Doing, as you are wise, you will tell us who shall speak with us, in behalf of all our Brothers the Americans.... as it is our earnest desire to remain in peace and friendship with our Br: the Americans for ever.[47]

---

45. Chickasaw Minkos to His Excellency the President of the Honorable Congress of the United States, 28 July 1783, in *Calendar of Virginia State Papers, Vol. III*, 515-517.

46. Cotterill, "Virginia-Chickasaw Treaty of 1783," 492.

47. Chickasaw Minkos to His Excellency the President of the Honorable Congress of the United States, 28 July 1783, in *Calendar of Virginia State Papers, Vol. III*, 516.

With the sudden American victory at Yorktown, they asked a fair question about the leadership and formation of the post-Revolutionary United States government. Several colonists, heads of state and nations, and others desired to know the same thing.

The Chickasaw delegates arrived at the October treaty site on time, but were delayed ten days waiting for Martin and Donelson to arrive. Despite Reid's invitation, the Delawares, Choctaws, and Creeks failed to participate. Instead of French Lick, the participants convened near a large sulphur spring on Richland Creek, several miles outside of the frontier settlement and close to the rural log cabin home of James Robertson. Today, a historical marker at the corner of Morrow Road and Terry Drive in a quiet residential neighborhood in west Nashville near West Park marks the site. Robertson's home later served as the first Chickasaw-Choctaw Agency when he served as its agent.[48]

The negotiations started on November 4 and finished two days later with the signing of the Virginia-Chickasaw Treaty of 1783 (sometimes referred to as the French Lick Treaty).[49] Chickasaw interpreter Malcom McGee served as the translator during the discussions.[50] Martin opened the conference by reading a letter from Governor Harrison. Donelson then spelled out Virginia's wishes. Tuskau Pautaupau (called the "Red King" in the treaty) provided the Chickasaw response, offering the Virginia negotiators a string of white beads as an everlasting symbol of the bond they sought with them and the new United States. He also credited Piominko for playing the key role in all the discussions leading up to this one. When they met the following day, both sides came to terms. The resulting treaty pledged peace between the Commonwealth of Virginia and the tribe and required the Chickasaws to remove some of the Delawares residing in their midst who remained hostile to the settlers. The commissioners, in return, agreed to help prevent further unwelcome settler encroachment in their lands, except for the invited traders. Both sides then agreed with Chickasaw claims that the northeastern Chickasaw land boundary ran from the "mouth of the Duck River to the mouth of the Tennessee River and the dividing ridge between the Tennessee and Cumberland as high as the Duck River." The new treaty did not include any land cessions, as Harrison and others desired. Piominko closed the meeting of delegates by saying:

> Peace is now settled, I was the first that proposed it, as to the differences that are settled, upon over lands I am very ready to remove them, and am in hope no more blood shed by either party which will give general satisfaction to my people and I hope to the Governors, I have no more to

---

48. Atkinson, *Splendid Land, Splendid People*, 122-123.
49. Cotterill, "Virginia-Chickasaw Treaty of 1783," 494.
50. Atkinson, *Splendid, Land, Splendid People*, 123.

say only wish the land to be observed that was spoken of
and claimed by the King.

His words confirm Tuskau Pautaupau's acknowledgment of his prime role in all the complicated discussions leading up to the treaty. He signed the document as "Tushatohoa The Mountain Leader." It appears likely that this is the manner Piominko chose to sign his name. If so, this reveals his original name prior to the more commonly used title name of Piominko.[51]

An expressed willingness by both sides to befriend one another and attempt to settle past differences proved to be an important starting point, but little else, as ongoing and complicated diplomatic challenges lie ahead. Perhaps more important than the document resulting from the meeting near French Lick was a budding friendship between Piominko and Robertson. The two first met in several discussions leading up to the final treaty negotiations. Throughout those discussions they developed a respect and fondness for each other. They remained close friends for the rest of their lives. As one will see in the chapters ahead, the evolution and importance of that friendship is easily documented and charted.

However, the details surrounding perhaps one of the earliest expressions of the bond between the two men remains somewhat clouded in the historical records. A relatively obscure book by Lizzie P. Elliott may offer some answers to a riddle relating to personal items that Piominko is alleged to have gifted Robertson as a sign of their budding friendship. Those items are now on display at the Tennessee State Museum.[52] In 1911 Elliott published an *Early History of Nashville*. Elliott's father, the Reverend Collins D. Elliott, served as a longtime educator at the Nashville Female Academy.[53] The academy, which was created in the Cumberland settlement's earliest years under a different name, was originally overseen by Robertson's sister, and several of Robertson's children attended school there.[54] Reverend Elliott started his career at the academy nearly fifty years later, but it is possible that some of the earliest records of the school and the settlement remained during his tenure, or at least stories of them did. It is also conceivable that as she grew up, Lizzie Elliot's father shared with her the stories he heard and his knowledge and insights into the relatively

---

51. Treaty at French Lick with the Chickasaws, November 6, 1783, at *Papers of the War Department, 1784-1800*, Center for History and New Media, http://wardepartmentpapers.org.

52. Sallie Norton of the General James Robertson Chapter of the Daughters of the American Revolution, email message to Mitch Caver, May 19, 2012; Ridley Willis II to Norton, May 18, 2012. Nashville historian and author Ridley Willis II deserves credit for pointing the authors to Elliott's book and the potential connection between Piominko and the gifts on display in the museum.

53. J.E. Windrow, "Collins D. Elliott and the Nashville Female Academy," *Tennessee Historical Magazine* 3 (1935): 74-106.

54. John Woodridge, ed., *History of Nashville* (Nashville, TN: H.W. Crew, by the Publishing House of the Methodist Episcopal Church, 1890), 405.

short history of the Nashville area they called home. Dedicating her book to her father, she states in her preface she wanted to ensure future generations knew the "stories" of the local history. In fanciful and sometimes romanticized language, Elliott wrote that at the close of the 1783 treaty convention Piominko addressed Robertson and offered him several symbolic gifts. First, he placed in his hand a leather string to demonstrate the strong bond of their friendship. Next, he handed Robertson a doeskin bag representing the trust the Chickasaws had in him to protect and safeguard their interests. Finally, he offered him a pair of moccasins that meant that where the "little Father" (as they called Robertson) led, the tribe would gladly follow. Elliott maintained that those items remained in Nashville at the time her book was published and were among the city's most treasured items.[55]

Today, the Tennessee State Museum in Nashville, appropriately located just off the James Robertson Parkway, has in its "Frontier" exhibit a beautifully exquisite and remarkably well-preserved ribbon trim and glass-beaded bag and a similarly decorated pair of moccasins. Some, including local Nashville historians, suggest these are likely Piominko's presents to his friend at the treaty grounds as mentioned in Elliott's book. Unfortunately, Elliott does not offer any citations throughout the book to document her information or her sources. She only maintains that much of the book is based on a synthesis of four known authors of her generation of Nashville or Tennessee history and her father and his love of history. While most of those authors mention the treaty at French Lick, none of them mention a gift exchange between Piominko and Robertson. In the course of writing her account, she also perpetuates mistakes by some of those historians by incorrectly noting the treaty occurred in June when it happened in November and that the Chickasaw Nation ceded land when they did not. While Robertson attended the meetings, no other documents or historians note that he spoke or addressed anyone.

Multiple searches today have failed to produce a second account to verify her story, and it was not mentioned in the official treaty documents, now filed in the War Department's records. In fact, they do not mention any role Robertson played in the final negotiations or any addresses he made to the assembled Chickasaw leaders. Since the gifts were perhaps of a personal nature between two individuals, and not offerings to the larger Virginia treaty party, the official records may have not recorded the transaction. An email exchange with Ron Westphal, curator of science and technology at the Tennessee State Museum, indicates the provenance of the items on display at the museum is unclear, but it is believed that the General James Robertson Chapter of the

---

55. Lizzie P. Elliott, *Early History of Nashville* (Nashville, TN: Ambrose Printing Company, 1911), 196-198.

Daughters of the American Revolution (DAR) donated them.[56] Unfortunately, the local DAR chapter today has no records of any of the donations or information on where the items originated. Smithsonian's *Handbook of North American Indians, Volume 14, Southeast* has a black and white photo of the moccasins with a caption that indicates "according to Robertson family tradition" these items were presented to Robertson by Piominko during the treaty negotiations in 1783.[57] The caption, however, fails to provide the source for that information. When Smithsonian collected the illustrations and information for their fine *Handbook of North American Indians*, because of the breadth of coverage and sheer size of the volumes, they often had to rely on local museums, repositories, and institutions and the specialists within them to provide the photos and the reason for their importance. If the Tennessee State Museum provided the photo of the pair of moccasins, they may have simply shared the long assumed account of their origins.

Joy O'Donnell, one of the archivists at the National Society of the Daughters of the American Revolution, provided some additional insight. Organizers created the General James Robertson Chapter in 1923, with several of his descendants as founding members. Since the local DAR chapter owned the Robertson items they later donated to the museum, they were not required to report it to the national society. Proceedings from DAR Tennessee State Conferences in 1930, 1931, and 1947 also offer significant clues. It appears that in 1930 the local DAR donated several Robertson items. The following year a Robertson descendant in Memphis gifted the museum more items. In 1947, the proceedings inventoried and detailed the earlier chapter donations, which included "one pair of Indian moccasin used in treaty ceremony," "one Indian bag, beaded, used in treaty ceremony," "beaded bag, presented to Charlotte Reeves Robertson (James' wife) by friendly Indians," and "one string of Indian beads with pendant used in treaty ceremony." The chapter loaned the articles to the Tennessee State Museum for the "purpose of preservation, education and historical value."[58] In the summer of 2012, Chickasaw Nation representative Regina Berna carefully examined the items and returned home impressed by their craftsmanship and their potential historical value. The verdict remains out, however, on their direct correlation to Piominko. While there is no conclusive evidence as to their origins, it appears likely they once belonged to him. When Piominko addressed a group gathered in Nashville just a few months after signing the Virginia-Chickasaw Treaty, he offered the American

---

56. Ron Westphal, email message to Mitch Caver, April 26, 2012.

57. Raymond Fogelson and William Sturtevant, eds., *Handbook of North American Indians, Vol. 14: Southeast* (Smithsonian Institution, September 20, 2004), 485.

58. Joy O'Donnell, email message to Mitch Caver, Feb 9, 2016

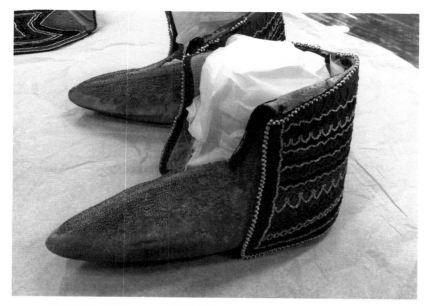

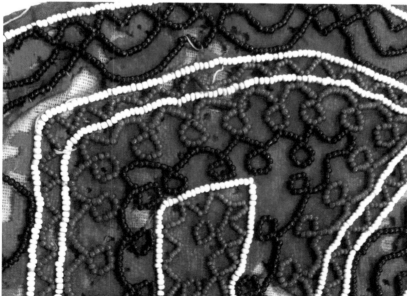

Top:
Beaded moccasins displayed at the Tennessee State Museum in Nashville could be the moccasins Piominko presented to General James Robertson during treaty negotiations in 1783.

Bottom:
A close-up of a glass-beaded bag on display at the Tennessee State Museum. Historians believe the bag could be the one Piominko presented to General Robertson's wife, Charlotte, in 1783. *Photos courtesy of Regina Cravatt Berna*

officials there beaded items as a symbol of their growing friendship.[59] He obviously saw this an important gesture. It is quite conceivable he did the same thing just a few months prior to this.

Regardless of the supposed authenticity of the museum items, something more valuable than beaded items transpired during those treaty negotiations and later bore priceless and immeasurable fruit. The growing friendship between Piominko and Robertson created a legacy that shaped both the Chickasaw Nation's course and the critical early history of the United States, and the effects of that partnership reverberate today. Both Robertson and Piominko were exceptionally talented, astute, effective, visionary, and determined individuals. Each of these new friends correctly concluded that a partnership offered the best hope for the future of both groups. Piominko summarized it best when he said that brothers never permanently split over disagreements, but they make friends again. They patch up their differences to ensure the prosperity of future generations.[60] In 1784, North Carolina legislators officially named the area that Robertson helped settle Nashborough, as originally planned. They later shortened it to Nashville.[61] It quickly developed into an important commercial center for that region.

It is likely that Nashville, the future state of Tennessee, the fledgling United States, and the Chickasaw Nation would have each survived without the efforts to forge partnerships that benefited all. However, it is interesting to ponder how the outcomes and the trajectory of each might have been changed had Piominko, Robertson, and the others chosen different paths in the delicate decisions they faced in 1783. Growing factionalism both within the Chickasaw Nation and the Congress of the Confederation, Spanish designs on land in the Southeast, and unsettled tribes in the Old Northwest threatening war over contested lands that threatened to spill over into the Cumberland River region all jeopardized the fragile peace. Yet today, more than two hundred years later, as Piominko and Robertson both hoped, their nations and their communities remain strong and prosperous.

In the years leading up to Piominko's leadership, his people had been forced to navigate immense economic change and disruption, imperial and colonial wars pressuring them to choose sides, and increased encroachments on their land. As the Revolutionary War drew to a close, the forces it had unleashed were by no means finished. In the midst of the war, Spain had decided that the civil war between colonists and the mother country afforded it the perfect opportunity to declare war on Britain and advance its own interests,

---

59. "The Substance of a Talk Held at Nashville with Some of the Chickasaws," in *The State Records of North Carolina, Vol. XVII, 1781-85*, ed. Walter Clark (Goldsboro, NC: 1899), 85-87.
60. Message from the Chickasaw, July 9, 1782, in *Calendar of Virginia State, Vol. III*, 278.
61. Putnam, *History of Middle Tennessee*, 202.

and the Spanish elicited the support of Native American allies to help them. With his commitment to America, Piominko turned his energies toward obstructing Spanish interests that threatened his allies and Chickasaw territories.

CHAPTER THREE

ADEPT NAVIGATOR

───•◦•───

"The character of the Indian chief [Piominko] inspires me with
hope that he will elude the efforts of his enemy."

- Virginia Governor Lee Henry in December 1791 expressing his optimism to
President George Washington that Piominko had survived the defeat of General
Arthur St. Clair's forces at Fort Washington weeks before, at the time Henry
wrote the letter Piominko remained unaccounted for

───•◦•───

WITH England's defeat in the American Revolution, America and Spain now grappled to protect, control, and advance their claims. The Mississippi valley became ground zero between the competing interests, and again the tribes in that area were caught in the middle. Certainly it was in the best interest of both Spain and the United States to court Native American allies to join their sides, and they pitched favorable terms to them. Grappling with the difficult and complex issues stemming from the powerful competing interests, Chickasaws began to factionalize. As the leader of one faction, Piominko quickly made up his mind, and his decision was clear: he would side with America.

Shortly before England's surrender at Yorktown in the fall of 1781, Spanish General Bernardo de Galvez, commander of the Spanish forces in North America, in a masterful military campaign captured British positions in present-day Louisiana and Mississippi. He then turned his attention to British-controlled Pensacola. With the combination of a large naval and ground assault, later known as the Battle of Pensacola, he placed the city under siege for two months. Despite Creek, Choctaw, and Chickasaw warriors rushing to aid Britain, Pensacola fell to Spain. Most of the Native American warriors returned home dejected and frustrated because they had not received the support and supplies necessary to defend the besieged city. De Galvez succeeded in effectively regaining both west and east Florida for Spain. As a result, Spain's control stretched along the Gulf Coast from New Orleans to Florida, and it exerted claims on territory from the mouth of the Yazoo River to the Ohio, which included Chickasaw lands.[1]

On the heels of that victory, in March of the following year, a pro-Spanish faction of the Chickasaw Nation traveled with representatives from the Shawnee, Delaware, and Cherokee Nations to offer four "blue and white belts" to Spanish officials in St. Louis. Seeking protection and an alliance, they offered these gifts as a peace gesture in the name of 130 tribes. The officials immediately reciprocated with presents to the leaders of the tribal participants as a token of friendship. In private correspondence between Spanish officials, they recognized the need to reach out to the Chickasaws and Cherokees in particular so that neither would obstruct traffic on the Mississippi River, and Spain would have unfettered use of it.[2]

Realizing a window of opportunity had opened, Governor Esteban Miro of Louisiana dispatched messengers to Chickasaw villages to cement the alliance. Miro knew that diplomacy represented his best option, and if he pursued a military plan to coerce them it would result in numerous Spanish casualties. He used the best political and diplomatic tool he had available to him and offered needed trade supplies. Miro's strategy partially worked. Paya Mattaha, a onetime staunch British ally, accepted Spain's olive branch and sought to establish a trade relationship. In 1784 the elderly Chickasaw leader traveled to Chickasaw Bluffs, where he suddenly died from an illness. On his deathbed, he told the Spanish officials he had admonished the young warriors to live in harmony with Spain. Representing the friendship, he supposedly asked to be buried in a Spanish flag.[3]

At nearly the same time, in June of 1784, 325 delegates representing six of the seven Chickasaw villages traveled nearly 600 miles round-trip to attend a Spanish conference at Mobile. They were accompanied by representatives from the Choctaws and Alabamas. The delegation, which ultimately consisted of representatives from seventy-three villages, was a diverse group that included leaders, warriors, elderly, and women and children. They sought guaran-

---

1. Colin G. Calloway, *The American Revolution in Indian Country: Crisis and Diversity in Native American Communities* (Cambridge: Cambridge University Press, 1995), 227-228.

2. Louis Houck, ed., *The Spanish Regime in Missouri, Vol. 1* (Chicago: Donnelley and Sons Company, 1909), 209-210.

3. Calloway, *The American Revolution in Indian Country*, 235.

Esteban Miro, Spanish governor of Louisiana, worked tirelessly to persuade the Chick-asaws to agree to an alliance with Spain. Coordinating his efforts with those of Creek leader Alexander McGillivray, he initially tried to pave the way to an alliance with gifts and favors, with limited success, before resorting to force, which also proved futile. *Esteban Rodriguez Miro, 1744-1795, courtesy of Louisiana State Museum, portrait by Andres Molinary 1916*

tees not just of trade, but of fair trade practices, and they wanted to discuss a mutually beneficial defense against American encroachments with the Spanish. Paya Mattaha's grandson served as an intermediary on behalf of Spain to persuade the Chickasaw Nation to participate.

Spain well understood the importance of the conference and went to great effort and expense to prepare for it. The Spanish hosts provided each participant with costly gifts that included commemorative medals, blankets, clothing, guns, tools, cooking utensils, cloth, yarn, and numerous other personal items.[4] The Chickasaw village of Chokka' Falaa' alone consumed nearly 1,000 pounds of bread and meat and more than that in rice. Collectively, the seven villages took home nearly 6,000 pounds of bread, 10,000 pounds of rice, and 2,400 pounds of beans, meat, and cornmeal. Additional medals were also given to the leaders.[5]

The Spanish officials' efforts with the Chickasaw representatives at Mobile allowed them to achieve their goals, but only temporarily. In the treaty of alliance that resulted from the conference, the Chickasaws agreed to release captive Spaniards, accept Spanish protection, pledge loyalty to the king of Spain, keep peace with neighboring tribes, and only accept Spanish traders. In return, Spain agreed to defend the Chickasaws, help them expel unwanted traders, and supply trade goods at a fair price. The latter they fulfilled almost immediately by facilitating the delivery of trade goods to the seven Chickasaw villages from Pensacola and Mobile.[6] While the treaty represented the wishes of some of the Chickasaw leaders it did not reflect those of others, including Piominko.

Spain effectively courted Piominko's Chickasaw rival, Wolf's Friend (also known as Ugulayacabe), by secretly paying him $500 annually for his loyalty. Piominko suspected the under-the-table remuneration.[7] Robertson, upon meeting Wolf's Friend, had called him "one of the greatest and influential characters in the Chickasaw Nation," "sensible," and said he "controlled three-fourths" of the tribe.[8] Large in stature, Wolf's Friend carried himself with poise and confidence and a sense of flair. At a conference in Nashville in 1792, he adorned himself in a European-style scarlet coat with silver lace

---

4. Lawrence Kinnaird, "Spanish Treaties with Indian Tribes," *The Western Historical Quarterly* 10, no. 1 (January 1979): 41-46.

5. Calloway, *The American Revolution in Indian Country*, 235; Kathleen DuVal, *Independence Lost: Lives on the Edge of the American Revolution* (New York: Random House, 2015), 261.

6. Arrell M. Gibson, *The Chickasaws* (Norman: University of Oklahoma Press, 1971), 77.

7. Calloway, *The American Revolution in Indian Country*, 329; James Atkinson, *Splendid Land, Splendid People: The Chickasaw Indians to Removal* (Tuscaloosa: University of Alabama Press, 2004), 173.

8. James Robertson to Pennington, 20 October 1798, in "Correspondence of General James Robertson," *The American Historical Magazine* 4, no. 1 (October 1899): 368-369.

and carried a nearly matching substantial silk umbrella. Likely close in age to Piominko, he called Chisha' Talla'a' (Post Oak Grove) home.[9] Located on Coonewah Creek, Wolf's Friend's village lay about six miles due west of Piominko's Chokka' Falaa' village. Like most Southeastern Indian communities, Chickasaw villages remained relatively independent of each other and were semi-autonomous, but would coalesce for ceremonies, events, and other matters of importance, such as national defense. Chisha' Talla'a' and Chokkilissa', which Chickasaw interpreter Malcolm McGee identified as "where the king resided," supported partnering with Spain, while Chokka' Falaa' preferred the Americans. These three larger villages had the most power, and the smaller villages generally sided with one or more of them.[10]

In terms of leadership, Wolf's Friend and Piominko came from very different backgrounds. Wolf's Friend descended from a ranking female member of a Chickasaw peace clan. He achieved his leadership status by virtue of an inherited birthright. Wolf's Friend probably was a warrior who went on to serve as a civil minko. His name of Ugulayacabe could represent a war title, Okla Ayaka' Abi' ("Slayer of Each Nation"), suggesting that he may have been a warrior early in his life.[11] However, to date, no records have been uncovered to document his participation in any military actions. Piominko achieved his status not by heredity or birthright, but the strength of his leadership skills. He rose through the ranks not as a peace or civil minko, but an accomplished military and diplomatic leader.[12] In many ways, the two couldn't have been more opposite. Not only had Piominko spent many of his early years growing up in a Cherokee village before returning to lead his people, his rise to leadership challenged the traditional route that many traveled previously to lead the Chickasaws. Piominko represented a new type of Chickasaw leader, where merit trumped birth and power politics. Remaining respectful of the hereditary minko, he often won them to his side with logic and powers of persuasion. Piominko and others like him were ushering in a new system for determining tribal leadership, replacing the age-old traditional one that had come before. External pressures brought by European outsiders began to elevate the status of war minkos over civil ones and the intruders also indirectly introduced new

---

9. Atkinson, *Splendid Land, Splendid People*, 128.

10. James R. Atkinson, "A Narrative Based on an Interview with Malcolm McGee by Lyman C. Draper," *Journal of Mississippi History* 66 (Spring 2004): 51. Throughout the eighteenth-century several Chickasaw minkos adopted the title of king as a direct result of European influences and referred to themselves with that designation. Atkinson, *Splendid Land, Splendid People*, 27.

11. John Dyson, email message to Tom Cowger, March 20, 2016.

12. John Dyson, *The Early Chickasaw Homeland: Origins, Boundaries and Society* (Ada, OK: Chickasaw Press, 2014), 85-86.

political systems in negotiations.[13]

There were numerous types of minkos, and they often fell into two categories: war minkos and peace/civil minkos. Simply meaning "leader," the title minko applied to many positions, minor or elevated. Each village, it appears, had its own minko. Several eighteenth- and nineteenth-century accounts detailed the ordinations of new hereditary peace/civil minkos and "kings," and they bore similarity one to another. With the passing of a minko, family and friends readied the ceremony to replace the deceased with his sister's oldest son. They built a new arbor on the village ceremonial grounds, where they danced and sang for extended periods of time over the course of four days. Early in the morning of the fourth day, they placed the designated new hereditary minko in a white chair created for that purpose. Placing a "pipe of peace" in his mouth, he faced east as the sun rose. Shortly thereafter, males circled the ceremonial grounds four times performing a peace dance. Warriors then carried him in the chair to a local water source, dunked him several times, and ceremonially bathed him. As he returned to his house, participants in the procession route threw corn stalks at him to "denote plenty." When they returned him to his house the formal ceremony ended, but dancing continued into the night. Having ritualistically cleansed him and celebrated his ordination, he was now prepared to assume control over the peace and harmony of his community. Unfortunately, these same sources reveal little about how leaders were chosen for lesser duties or the ceremonies conducted on their behalf. Since almost everything was ritualized to some degree, those selections must have been as well, and some type of ordination ceremony must have occurred when an individual received a new title.[14]

By the early eighteenth century, European-introduced systems had eroded the sanctity of the hereditary minko position, as many of those same civil leaders coveted trade goods provided by the deerskin trade and slave trafficking. They willingly spilled blood for them, contrary to the rules of inheritance. As a result of the corrosion of the position and the constant state of conflict brought by competing European powers, hereditary minkos had lost most of their power by 1700 and war minkos challenged the peace/civil minkos for increased stature. Certainly Chickasaw "kings" had little of the political power of most of their European counterparts, and their positions were not compa-

---

13. Ibid., 86-87.

14. Captain Thomas Nairne, *Nairne's Muskhogean Journals: The 1708 Expedition to the Mississippi River*, ed. by Alexander Moore (Jackson: University of Mississippi Press, 1988), 38-41; Robert Boyte C. Howell, *The Baptist, Vol. IV* (Nashville: W.H. Dunn, 1838), 238-239; John Dyson, email message to Tom Cowger, March 20, 2016.

rable.[15] Thus, the rivalry between Wolf's Friend and Piominko was not simply one between adversaries who shared differing views on whether to side with America or Spain, but also one of tribal political practices and the hereditary rights of matrilineal clans. The stakes between the two were high and occasionally so was the friction between them. While Piominko and Wolf's Friend often shared different views and the means to achieve them, in the end they both sought the best future for the Chickasaw Nation.

Chickasaw Minko Taski Etoka (Tashka Alhtoka', "Appointed Warrior") closely partnered with Wolf's Friend. Non-Natives referred to the former as the Hare Lip King.[16] Like Wolf's Friend he was a hereditary minko who rose to power following the death of his uncle, Minko Houma, the Red King, in 1784. Some outsiders who knew him described him as easily duped, lazy, rude, and easily bribed, while others said he was shrewd, tireless, and dedicated. Perhaps the truth lies somewhere in the middle, but in light of the contradiction one must also question the motives of those who described him (particularly those who described him negatively), their dealings with him, and why they may have said what they did. Regardless, he logged countless miles on behalf of the Chickasaws, and his passion for the future of his people came out at some of the conferences he attended.[17]

While Spain optimistically hoped the meetings at St. Louis and Mobile and the support of Wolf's Friend and Taski Etoka represented the dawn of an important new partnership with the Chickasaws, Piominko soon dashed their aspirations and held a different course. Nearly a year after the gathering at Mobile, Piominko and several other Chickasaw leaders traveled to the state of Franklin to meet with its newly appointed governor, John Sevier, at his home on the Nolichucky River, in present-day northeastern Tennessee. Traveling as far north as Long Island of the Holston, near present-day Kingston, Tennessee, Piominko sought trade and an alliance to thwart potential threats from the Creeks. In return, he promised to provide protection against pillaging Cherokee parties who made trade difficult up and down the Tennessee River.[18]

The state of Franklin represented a short-lived attempt by separatists in ceded lands in North Carolina to create an independent government in 1784. Anxious settlers and land entrepreneurs in Washington, Sullivan, and Greene counties of North Carolina created Franklin when North Carolina offered to relinquish land in its western reaches, located today in far northeastern Ten-

---

15. Nairne, *Nairne's Muskhogean Journals*, 38-39, 41; John Dyson, email message to Tom Cowger, March 20, 2016.

16. Dyson, *The Early Chickasaw Homeland*, 146.

17. Atkinson, *Splendid Land, Splendid People*, 127.

18. Samuel C. Williams, *History of the Lost State of Franklin* (New York: Press of the Pioneers, 1933), 264.

nessee, to the United States to help pay off its American Revolutionary War debts. They chose Jonesborough as their capital, set up a provisional government, declared independence from North Carolina, and sought admittance as the fourteenth state. Franklin framers elected John Sevier as governor and cited neglect, taxation, distance, and lack of representation as the reason behind their separation from North Carolina. By early 1789 the secession movement lost energy, its organizers abandoned their hopes for statehood, and the land reverted back to North Carolina. In time North Carolina ceded it once again to Congress to form the Southwest Territory, which would eventually become the state of Tennessee, and John Sevier would serve as its first governor.[19]

Sevier and James Robertson were close associates and leaders of the Watauga Association, and Piominko undoubtedly visited Sevier while he was Franklin's governor at Robertson's suggestion. The two also developed a friendship, and in later correspondence, Sevier affectionately referred to Piominko as his "brother."[20] Sevier was not the only one impressed by Piominko on his visit to the state of Franklin, and everywhere he stopped he received a warm reception. The first daily newspaper in the United States, *The Pennsylvania Packet* published in Philadelphia, printed a letter from an observer on the influence Piominko had when he met him on the trip.[21] The editorialist wrote:

> He seemed to be a man endowed with more than ordinary prowess of mind and humanity; for an Indian. In his speeches, he delivered himself fluently and with great force of argument, disclosing a clear knowledge of the strength and interest of the Southern tribes, and of the causes and effect of the late Revolution. These people (the Chickasaws) are more comely in their persons and kindlier in their dispositions than any of the nations I have been acquainted with.[22]

Piominko and the group of Chickasaw leaders that supported him then traveled to Hopewell Plantation, home of General Andrew Pickens, on the Keowee River in South Carolina, at the request of newly appointed US treaty commissioners Pickens, Benjamin Hawkins, Joseph Martin, and Lachlan

---

19. Michael Toomey, "State of Franklin," *NorthCarolinahistory.org: An Online Encyclopedia*, North Carolina History Project, at http://northcarolinahistory.org/encyclopedia/state-of-franklin/ (accessed February 9, 2016); Michael Toomey, "State of Franklin," in *Tennessee Encyclopedia of History and Culture*, University of Tennessee Press, January 2010, http://www.tennesseeencyclopedia.net/entry.php?rec=509.

20. John Sevier to Piomingo, or Mountain Leader, 15 December 1788, in *The State Records of North Carolina, Vol. XXII*, ed. Walter Clark, (Goldsboro, NC: 1907), 704-705.

21. Library of Congress, "Eighteenth Century American Newspapers in the Library of Congress," July 19, 2010, http://www.loc.gov/rr/news/18th/617.html.

22. Quoted in Williams, *Lost State of Franklin*, 264.

McIntosh. Cherokee, Creek, and Choctaw representatives attended separate conferences. En route, Creek and Cherokee war parties stole both Chickasaw and Choctaw horses and supplies while they camped.[23] The brazen attack demonstrated the difficulty the commissioners faced in trying to convene the meetings and keep peace between groups often hostile to each other.

Piominko addressed the four commissioners, offered them eight strands of white beads as a symbol of peace and friendship, and promised to keep his remarks short. He confidently informed them of his influence and status as he pointed to a medal he wore around his neck.

> You see this now, it was worn by our great man; he is dead;
> his daughter sent it for you to see it. I take place, as head
> leading warrior of the nation, to treat with all nations.[24]

Piominko's carefully worded remarks advised them that following Minko Houma's passing his influential family recognized Piominko as the most powerful war and diplomatic leader of the Chickasaw Nation. Taski Etoka participated in the meeting as the civil minko of the Chickasaw Nation. Piominko asked the commissioners to read the treaty, which had been prepared in advance, out loud, twice. In particular, he paid close attention to it the second time to ensure his requested revisions had been made. The sixteen-article Chickasaw treaty signed at Hopewell on January 10, 1786, reflected a compromise between Chickasaw and United States interests. It clarified Chickasaw boundaries, including defining the previously ambiguous Chickasaw eastern boundary line with the Choctaw Nation, declared Chickasaw loyalty to the United States, provided for trade between the two nations and the removal of uninvited traders, and expressed a shared desire for peace, and friendship. It also called for prisoner exchanges, although Piominko explained that he had no US prisoners to return because the Chickasaw Nation had not fought America. The treaty bore a striking resemblance to the one Wolf's Friend's faction signed with the Spanish at Mobile, but this time it partnered the Chickasaws to the United States, in effect creating a house divided.[25] The Cherokees and Choctaws signed similar but separate treaties with the Americans at Hopewell at different times.

Generally strongly opposed to land sales, Piominko agreed in the third article of the Hopewell treaty to an American request to use a tract of land to build a trading post on the lower part of the Muscle Shoals at the mouth of the Ocochappo (Bear Creek). Cherokee and Chickasaw leaders often clashed over disputed land at Muscle Shoals. To ensure that the land in question was no

---

23. DuVal, *Independence Lost*, 307.

24. Hopewell, 7 January 1786, *American State Papers: Indian Affairs* 1: 51.

25. Treaty With the Chickasaw, 10 January 1786, in *Indian Affairs: Laws and Treaties, Vol II*, ed. Charles J. Kappler (Washington, DC : Government Printing Office, 1904), 10-12.

larger than five miles in diameter, Piominko personally marked the area on a map provided him. He then agreed to permit future traders at the post to graze or cultivate lands near the marked area and immediately north of the river.[26] He made it clear that he had not ceded the land, but granted them use of it. Historian and archaeologist James Atkinson points out that the area Piominko designated for the post's construction is actually at the mouth of Ocochappo Creek (present-day Bear Creek) on a bend in the Tennessee River. It is close to the former town of Eastport, Mississippi, and the present-day northwestern border of Alabama and Mississippi.[27] Ironically, the United States never built the post. In time, Piominko protested its construction as circumstances changed following the treaty negotiations. He correctly claimed a few years later that its creation would lead to needless violence and open warfare with the Creek Nation.[28] George Colbert later built a profitable ferry and stand not far from the site.

The relatively innocuous-sounding second article of the treaty created a number of unforeseen problems for the Chickasaws as unscrupulous land-grabbers took advantage of it. The article stated that the treaty brought the Chickasaw Nation "under the protection of the United States of America, and no other sovereign whosoever."[29] When Piominko and the two other Chickasaw headmen signed the document, they likely did so to demonstrate their willingness to partner with America and not Spain as others wanted. They did not anticipate the greed of those who would use that clause to sell Chickasaw lands. Within three years of the treaty, US land developers advertised in Maryland a hundred acres of Chickasaw lands near present-day Memphis for $13.50, plus traveling expenses. The agents hawking the land argued that the receptive and peaceful nature of the Chickasaws in that region, and their distance from the lands being sold, paved the way for settlement.[30] In essence, the developers falsely claimed Chickasaws welcomed American immigration onto their lands. Nothing could have been further from the truth, and Piominko had not encouraged or authorized the sale of Chickasaw lands. Neither did he forfeit Chickasaw sovereignty to the United States.

As the treaty commission drew to a close, Piominko expressed his concern that the Creeks continued to plunder and kill "white people on the Cumberland and their property were equally dear to him with his own."[31] If those attacks continued on Chickasaw lands and targeted his friends, he promised

---

26. Ibid., 12.
27. Atkinson, *Splendid Land, Splendid People*, 129, 131.
28. Ibid., 129-130.
29. Treaty With the Chickasaw, 10 January 1786, *Indian Affairs: Laws and Treaties*, 12.
30. DuVal, *Independence Lost*, 308.
31. Hopewell, 7 January 1786, American State Papers: Indian Affairs 1: 52.

an appropriate response even though his nation would be outnumbered. The treaty at Hopewell pledged peace and friendship between the United States and Chickasaws and stated that "the hatchet shall be forever buried."[32] Piominko and those with him received treaty gifts from the commissioners and money to help purchase supplies. As the Chickasaw contingent left Hopewell, a band of Cherokees ambushed them, stole some of their horses, and robbed Piominko of his gifts and goods. Upon hearing the news, the commissioners immediately offered a reward for helping to retrieve the stolen items and bringing the culprits to justice. The following day the chief of the Chatuga (Chattooga) Cherokee, accompanied by three young men, returned the stolen items. Suggesting that he was unable to catch those responsible, he collected the reward.[33]

When the Creek attacks on Cumberland settlers living on Chickasaw lands continued, Piominko and other Chickasaw leaders grew restless. In a letter they sent to Governor Sevier just months after the Hopewell treaty, they wanted to know what actions the state of Franklin intended to take to stop the raids. In addition to the Creeks, they also blamed Chickamauga Cherokees for the recent deaths of several American settlers on Chickasaw lands on the Ohio River. They reminded the governor that Piominko had met with him the previous summer, and they were under the impression he would take action against these types of attacks. Not mincing words, the Chickasaws now wanted to know if Sevier planned to destroy the Creeks and Chickamaugas, or to patronize and tolerate their murdering and pillaging against the governor's own people.[34] But little was done to stop the assaults. So when an opportunity unexpectedly presented itself, Piominko took action, keeping his Hopewell vow to protect American settlers near Chickasaw boundaries.

In 1786, two Chickasaw hunters stumbled across a hidden village near present-day Tuscumbia, Alabama. Populated by renegade bands of Creeks, Cherokees, and Chickamaugas (Lower Cherokee), as well as a handful of French settlers, the village was called Cold Water. So named because of its close proximity to a large, cold stream that flowed from a limestone rock outcropping, the village site may have been located near present-day Spring Park in Tuscumbia. When the Cold Water villagers invited the two hunters to spend the night, they confided in them that they used their location as a base to carry out raids on the Cumberland settlers. The following morning the two Chicka-

---

32. Treaty With the Chickasaw, 10 January 1786, *Indian Affairs: Laws and Treaties*, 12.
33. Hopewell, 7 January 1786, American State Papers: Indian Affairs 1: 52.
34. "Talk from the kings, chiefs and leaders of the Chickasaw Nation, sent to John Sevier, Esquire, Governor of Franklin, 1786," Document: TCC212, Southeastern Native American Documents, 1730-1842, A GALILEO Digital Library of Georgia Database. Accessed February 14, 2016.

saw hunters raced to find Piominko to relay the news to him. They found him at Chickasaw Bluffs, near present-day Memphis, Tennessee. Once the hunters had rested, he immediately sent them to deliver the news to Colonel Robertson at the Cumberland settlement. Robertson wasted no time in raising a militia of 120 well-armed men. The two Chickasaw warriors who delivered the news led Robertson and his militia to the Cold Water village. After days of traveling they found the village on a rise a few hundred yards west of the creek. Catching the villagers off guard, Robertson's party killed many of them and took the others as prisoners, whom they later released. They recovered items the villagers had stolen from them in their raids and then burned the village to the ground. Robertson rewarded the two Chickasaw guides with a horse each and part of the recovered property, which they brought with them on their return trip to find Piominko. While the destruction of the village temporarily slowed the raids on the Cumberland settlers, it didn't completely stop them.[35]

The ink had barely dried on the treaties signed at Hopewell when a pro-Spanish coalition of tribal members, including Chickasaw supporters, led by mixed-blood Creek leader Alexander McGillivray (Hoboi-Hili-Miko) opposed the agreements. McGillivray, about the same age as Piominko, grew up at his prominent Scottish father's trading post near an Upper Creek village on the Little Tallassee River (also known as Little Tallase), not far from present-day Wetumka, Alabama. His mother was of Creek and French descent. Though McGillivray was educated at an English school in Charleston, his mother's Wind Clan ensured that he spoke the Muscogee language and learned Creek cultural traditions. His father's property was confiscated by revolutionaries for his service to Britain during the American Revolution. Hating Americans for seizing his father's property, McGillivray sought to create an alliance of southern tribes to force the United States out of Georgia, Kentucky, and Tennessee. When he signed the Treaty of Pensacola in 1784, McGillivray committed the Creek Nation to a trade agreement with Spain, and in return they made him a colonel and paid him fifty dollars a month for his services. The Spanish also sent him munitions for his assaults on Americans from the Cumberland Valley to Georgia. While he orchestrated the campaigns, McGillivray rarely fought in them. He also learned to play Euro-American powers off each other. When President George Washington persuaded McGillivray to journey to New York in 1790, he renounced his early treaty with Spain and signed a new agreement with the United States that made him a brigadier general with a salary of one hundred dollars a month. Shortly after returning home from his trip, he repudiated the Treaty of New York and signed a new treaty with Spain for $2,000 a

---

35. Edward Albright, *Early History of Middle Tennessee* (Nashville: Brandon Publishing Company, 1909), 131-135.

year, which was later raised to $3,500.

Spanish influence at the time relied heavily upon Panton, Leslie and Company traders operating out of New Orleans, Mobile, and Pensacola. Established in 1783 by Scottish merchants, the company quickly monopolized trade with Southeastern tribes. When Britain lost the Revolutionary War, Spain intended to boot the company out. Instead, realizing they lacked seasoned Spanish traders to fill the void, they partnered with them. McGillivray's Scottish descent, his mother's powerful clan affiliation, his disdain for the United States, and his strong influence in the Creek Nation made him an ideal ally for Spain and the trade company. Hoping to drive out their competitors, company management and agents pressed the tribes they traded with to resist American settlements and efforts to purchase tribal lands.[36] While McGillivray interacted with all the Spanish and company officials, he remained the closest with William Panton.

McGillivray died February 16, 1793, from gout and pneumonia while on a trip to Pensacola. His friends buried him with Masonic rites in a backyard garden of William Panton's plantation home. By the time of his death, McGillivray had accumulated great wealth acting as a clever business emissary for multiple and sometimes competing interests.[37]

Spain had no greater Native American ally than McGillivray, and Piominko had no greater nemesis or rival. Prior to his death, McGillivray challenged Piominko multiple times and called him "a very troublesome fellow."[38] McGillivray first opposed Piominko in 1786 over his land transaction at the mouth of Ocochappo Creek (Bear Creek). He incorrectly maintained that Piominko had ceded access to land that belonged to the Creeks. McGillivray argued that Piominko's misrepresentation of Chickasaw ownership of that land gave his nation the right to drive off or exterminate settlers who attempted to construct the trading post there.[39] McGillivray accused Piominko of accepting bribes from American officials to part with the land and said that they had duped him. McGillivray was wrong on both accounts. The Creeks did not own the land in question, and Piominko only received the customary treaty gifts presented at those types of conferences.[40] Piominko's desire to have the commissioners read the treaty out loud twice, his detailed questions, and his preciseness in drawing the boundaries of the land in question on the treaty map,

---

36. Herbert J. "Jim" Lewis, "Panton, Leslie & Company," in *Encyclopedia of Alabama*, last updated May 29, 2014; http://www.encyclopediaofalabama.org/article/h-3049#sthash.l84AbXec.dpuf.

37. John Walton Caughey, *McGillivray of the Creeks* (Norman: University of Oklahoma Press, 1938), 3, 9-12, 16, 25, 44, 53, 56.

38. McGillivray to Miro, 24 June 1789, in Caughey, *McGillivray of the Creeks*, 239.

39. Calloway, *The American Revolution in Indian Country*, 236.

40. Atkinson, *Splendid Land, Splendid People*, 131-133.

shows he knew exactly what he was doing and was not deceived. Tensions between Piominko's Chickasaw faction and McGillivray's Creek Confederacy continued to rise. Followers of Wolf's Friend kept McGillivray and Spain apprised of Piominko's movements and actions.[41]

Nearly a year after signing the Hopewell treaty, Piominko grew agitated that American officials had not kept their promises. In a letter to one of the commissioners, he complained that the United States had not delivered pledged trade goods and warned that Spain was more than willing to fill the void if America didn't. He then questioned the sincerity of the United States concerning the treaty and stated that perhaps the real purpose of it was "to jockey us out of our lands." If the promised trade goods didn't arrive, he maintained, the Chickasaws would be forced to "look for new friends." He then vowed to have a couple of his warriors deliver "a large belt of wampum" as a show of good faith and asked that they respond in kind to demonstrate they intended to keep the treaty provisions.[42]

When Piominko agreed to an American post at Chickasaw Bluffs a few months later, the newly elected Congress showed their appreciation by sending medals to the headmen and flags for their villages. They also agreed to send him weapons to counter Creek threats.[43] While Piominko's entourage probably only numbered around a hundred, McGillivray felt threatened by him.[44] McGillivray immediately decided upon a measured response to the perceived danger that Piominko and his supporters posed. He chose to target a small community of Georgian traders led by William Davenport and authorized by the Georgia legislature. Recently appointed by the Americans as Indian Commissioner for both the Chickasaw and Choctaw Nations, Davenport had located near a Chickasaw village at Chickasaw Bluffs on the Wolf River in 1786. The Chickasaws strategically placed some outposts near the bluffs to secure their western edge and protect vital interests on the Mississippi River. Within months of creating his post at Chickasaw Bluffs, Davenport warned Georgia Governor Edward Telfair of the urgent need to speed the delivery of goods to Chickasaw villages or risk losing them to the Spanish. He emphasized Spain's willingness and intent to undermine America's fragile relationship with the Chickasaw Nation.[45] Hoping to maintain Chickasaw loyalty, Davenport distributed gifts and medals to Piominko and other Chickasaw leaders. Span-

41. Gibson, *The Chickasaws*, 83.

42. Piomingo to Joseph Martin, 15 February 1787, in *Calendar of Virginia Papers, Vol. IV*, ed. William P. Palmer (Richmond: R.U. Derr Superintendent of Public Printing, 1884), 241-242.

43. Calloway, *The American Revolution in Indian Country*, 236-237.

44. Ibid., 237.

45. "William Davenport Letter, 1786 Nov. 1, Cumberland [to the] Governor [of] Georgia," Document: TCC211, Southeastern Native American Documents, 1730-1842, A GALILEO Digital Library of Georgia Database.

ish Governor Miro immediately took action and told McGillivray to pressure Chickasaw leaders to return the medals, oust Davenport and his colleagues, and cease trading with Americans.[46]

McGillivray went a step beyond Miro's instructions. Viewing Davenport's settlement as a violation of the treaty at Mobile, he dispatched warriors to destroy it and send a clear message to Piominko that he would not tolerate further American encroachment. While the Georgians were constructing buildings and possibly a fort in the settlement, the war party rode in and killed Davenport and six others, and wounded nearly as many. They also took a young German boy as a prisoner. Astonished bystanders stood speechless and helpless. The Creek-led war party departed for home, deliberately passing through Chickasaw villages to show off the scalps and seventy weapons they had taken in the raid. McGillivray had not consulted Spanish officials before the brutal attacks and later told them the ends justified the means. When they received the news, the Spanish officials worried about the gruesome manner in which McGillivray had disposed of the traders and expressed concerns that it might prompt American retaliation.[47] Following the assault, McGillivray sent messengers to Chickasaw and Choctaw communities demanding to know which side they were on, his or the American intruders. At the same time, he requested that Governor Miro not send Spanish supplies to those communities as punishment if they did not choose the right side. Shortly after the brazen attack on Davenport, McGillivray's Creek warriors returned from attacks on the Cumberland settlers, riding under the banner of a Spanish flag.[48] Piominko viewed the assaults against those settlers he hoped to protect as personal and exceptionally frustrating. It paled in comparison, though, to the intimate pain that McGillivray would soon inflict on him.

McGillivray began having Creek warriors patrol the routes between Chickasaw villages and American settlements in an effort to ensure they did not intend to violate the Treaty of Mobile. They often harassed and detained, occasionally robbed, and sometimes killed travelers on the trails. In the summer of 1789, McGillivray's sentinels ambushed and killed two Chickasaw couriers on assignment to deliver messages from Piominko to federal officials in the nation's capital. The attack occurred in the morning on the west side of the Clinch River and not far from the Cumberland settlements. It likely happened near present-day Kingston, Tennessee, where the Clinch empties into the Tennessee River. US District Judge John McNairy, who had recently been assigned to that area, and several whites traveling in the caravan, escaped by swimming

---

46. Gibson, *The Chickasaws*, 84.

47. McGillivray to O'Neil, 25 July 1787, and McGillivray to Miro, 4 October 1787, in Caughey, *McGillivray of the Creeks*, 158-162.

48. DuVal, *Independence Lost*, 309; Calloway, *The American Revolution in Indian Country*, 237.

across the Clinch. In their efforts to flee, they lost most of their horses and possessions.[49] When the marauders went through the personal belongings of the dead, they soon realized they had killed Piominko's brother, Long Hair (Panss Fallayah, or Ipashi Fala), and nephew. Upon receiving the letters Piominko sent to American officials, McGillivray told Governor Miro that they contained proof of Piominko's unwavering loyalty to the United States and his willingness to allow a post to be built at Chickasaw Bluffs. Convinced that the Chickasaws had now clearly chosen to side against him, McGillivray promised to destroy them for not joining his confederacy allied with Spain.[50] Not terribly concerned by the death of Piominko's family members, McGillivray reassured Panton that the Chickasaw Nation would not retaliate because Piominko lacked the support for it. He maintained instead that this served as an effective warning as to the consequences of challenging his confederacy and of refusing to side with Spain.[51] He boastfully warned that if Piominko's nation were foolhardy enough to seek revenge, they "will soon be destroyed."[52] McGillivray's statements couldn't have been further from the truth. When Piominko received word of the death of his brother and nephew, he vowed retaliation and revenge. The quarrel between Piominko and McGillivray soon escalated into open warfare.

Likely reeling from his loss and seething, Piominko knew his warriors lacked the manpower and munitions to launch a retaliatory strike. Had he chosen to seek immediate revenge, as he was surely tempted to do, it would have been extremely costly and futile. Instead, he demonstrated remarkable restraint and patience, waiting until he had the necessary strength to level the playing field and enact his desired retribution.

Traveling with other Chickasaw minkos and two whites, Piominko set off in September of 1789, a few months after the murders, to see "the Great Warrior at New York," President Washington. He planned to meet with the president at his executive mansion. Creek warriors attacked his party on the way to see the president, and Piominko barely escaped.[53] En route, he stayed with friends at Long Island of the Holston in far eastern Tennessee, near present-day Kingsport. These were acquaintances he had met on his trip to the state of Franklin a few years earlier. While there, he spoke with Cherokee

---

49. John Haywood, *The Civil and Political History of the State of Tennessee from its Earliest Settlement up to the Year 1796, Including the Boundaries of the State* (Nashville: Publishing House of the Methodist Episcopal Church, South, 1891), 256.

50. McGillivray to Miro, 24 June 1789, in Caughey, *McGillivray of the Creeks*, 239; Gibson, *The Chickasaws*, 84.

51. McGillivray to Panton, 10 August 1789, in Caughey, *McGillivray of the Creeks*, 248.

52. DuVal, *Independence Lost*, 337.

53. Colton Storm, ed., "Up the Tennessee in 1790: The Report of Major John Doughty to the Secretary of War," *East Tennessee Historical Society Publication* 17 (1945), 125.

Indian agent General Joseph Martin. Piominko had dealt with him several times, including during negotiations for the Virginia-Chickasaw Treaty of 1783 (Treaty of French Lick), where Martin served as one of the commissioners. He wanted Martin to deliver a letter he had written to North Carolina Governor Samuel Johnston. The letter asked the governor to allow Piominko to purchase two thousand pounds of gunpowder and bullets. He offered to pay for it with "skins, furs or horses." He also hoped they would lend military support. Without mentioning his brother and nephew by name, he referenced the murders and said that he was "determined to take Satisfaction for it."[54]

By mid-October, Piominko and his entourage reached Richmond, Virginia. Inclement weather forced them to abandon their plans to continue their journey to New York to meet with the president. Instead, Piominko decided to take his plea for munitions to Virginia Governor Beverley Randolph and the Virginia General Assembly. He forcefully reminded the Virginia government of its treaty obligations under the Virginia-Chickasaw Treaty of 1783. The assembly agreed to provide him with the requested powder and bullets and sent the president a note to inform him of their decision. They expressed to the president confidence in the new resolution they reached and felt that the commander in chief and Congress would agree with it. Equally important, they conveyed their assurance that the president would concur and repay the state for the cost of the supplies.[55] Piominko decided to leave the munitions at Long Island on the Holston in Tennessee for fear that he would be ambushed on the way home, as had happened on the trip out. Officials there promised to deliver the munitions to him when it was safer to transport them.[56] On Piominko's trip home, his party visited Kentucky and received additional munitions with the approval of Virginia officials, but to his great frustration he failed to secure a commitment of American soldiers for the pending war with the Creeks.[57]

At exactly the same time, Cumberland settlers in the Southwest Territory penned a letter to President Washington requesting that he supply Piominko with the munitions he desired. They did not know of Piominko's aborted trip to see the president and that he had switched gears and presented his request for munitions in Virginia. The settlers cited recent McGillivray-led attacks on them and the amiable relationship Piominko had with the United States as justification to support his request. These raids caused tremendous consternation as communities along the Cumberland River lived in a state of perpetual

---

54. "A talk delivered [to] Genl Joseph Martin by Piamingo chief warrior of the Chickasaw Nation... for His Excellency Samuel Johnson governor of the state of North Carolina [manuscript]: Long Island of the Holston, 1789 Sept. 28," Newberry Library, Edward E. Ayer Collection, American Indian Histories and Cultures Collection, Adam Matthews Digital.

55. Atkinson, *Splendid Land, Splendid People*, 134.

56. Storm, "Up the Tennessee in 1790," 125.

57. Atkinson, *Splendid Land, Splendid People*, 135.

fear of the next strike. The settlers warned of an upcoming war between the Creeks and Chickasaws and said if Piominko did not receive the desired weapons from the Americans, he would be forced to marry himself to the Spanish or the Creek Confederacy to survive. That outcome, they protested, would be disastrous for all involved. Piominko, they maintained, offered the best hope to stop the attacks, but he needed to be well-armed to do it.

Washington's secretary of war, Henry Knox, immediately responded to the letter on behalf of the president. He reassured the settlers that although Piominko did not make the planned trip to see the president in New York that fall, the Virginia legislature had authorized the munitions and furnished them to him at Richmond. Both the United States and Piominko could claim victory, and it demonstrated their important symbiotic relationship. Piominko had the munitions he needed to seek retribution and protect his nation, and America had an indispensable ally that could help protect its citizens in the Cumberland Valley, as well as slow the interests of Spain and its Creek Confederacy allies led by McGillivray.[58]

In April 1790, Henry Knox and President Washington sent Major John Doughty on a fact-finding mission to visit the tribes south of the Ohio River and ascertain their receptiveness to American trade. Traveling up the Tennessee River, he made a deliberate stop at the Chickasaw communities. While there he visited with Piominko, his brother Alaitamoto, and eight influential warriors who told him that they were in desperate need of promised trade goods ranging from munitions to clothing. Not understanding the delays, Piominko reminded him that the Chickasaw and Choctaw Nations were the only ones that had demonstrated continual friendship with the Americans. He and his brother then forcefully reminded Doughty that since the treaty at Hopewell they had received nothing but promises. In particular, Piominko noted the supplies he left at Long Island on the Holston still hadn't arrived six months later. Doughty took note and recorded the "distressed" plight of the Chickasaws when he visited them. He made clear to Knox and Washington that the Chickasaw Nation is no longer interested in hollow promises, but action. Doughty made arrangements with Piominko to meet three or four Chickasaws and Choctaws the following month, on May 9, at the falls on the Ohio River to deliver the much-needed powder and bullets. Doughty maintained that was the earliest date Piominko could meet him. After the rendezvous, Doughty vowed that soldiers would escort the party by boat and on horseback to en-

---

58. "To George Washington from the inhabitants of Kentucky, 8 September 1789 [letter not found]," *Founders Online*, National Archives, last modified December 28, 2016, http://founders.archives.gov/documents/Washington/05-04-02-0002. [Original source: *The Papers of George Washington*, Presidential Series, vol. 4, *8 September 1789–15 January 1790*, ed. Dorothy Twohig. Charlottesville: University Press of Virginia, 1993, pp. 2–3.]

sure that the carriers safely delivered the munitions to the Chickasaw villages and were not ambushed en route. Piominko assured Doughty that he would deliver that message to the Choctaws.[59] Nearly six months later Doughty delivered a personal letter to Piominko from President Washington assuring him that the bonds between the nations were robust and that they would honor the Treaty of Hopewell. He then comforted him that he and other American officials had no interest in Chickasaw lands. The latter proved untrue.[60] When the letter arrived, however, Washington's assurances were words that Piominko needed to hear, as forces swirled that threatened an already divided Chickasaw Nation.

While Piominko struggled to secure the promised and much-needed supplies and to prepare for a rapidly approaching conflict with McGillivray and the Creeks, Spain continued to make inroads with others in the Chickasaw Nation through the influence of the previously mentioned Panton, Leslie and Company traders. Their field agents resided in the Chickasaw villages and those of other neighboring tribes. McGillivray pressed Louisiana and West Florida Governor Francisco Luis Hector, barón de Carondelet to embed Spanish agents and traders within Chickasaw country for the purpose of quietly dividing the nation in order to conquer it.[61]

William Panton and others visited Piominko in 1790 to determine his commitment to the United States and his standing within the Chickasaw Nation. Panton left convinced that Piominko intended to permit an American post on the Tennessee River, but wrongly concluded that Taski Etoka held more sway in the tribe and through his influence the Chickasaws would fully partner with Spain.[62] While Piominko traveled to Virginia in search of munitions for his upcoming war with the Creeks, General James Wilkinson visited Long Town. Wilkinson, a former Revolutionary War hero, had dishonored himself as a double agent by 1787 and was secretly on Spain's payroll advancing their interests and his own. After the trip to the Chickasaw village, he encouraged Governor Miro to persuade McGillivray "to have this troublesome fellow [Piominko] cut off."[63] Whether Wilkinson's menacing suggestion implied assassination is unclear. Regardless, Spanish officials, Panton, Leslie and Company, and McGillivray closely monitored him. Instead of intimidating him, they only nudged him closer to his American allies.

Wolf's Friend, on the other hand, responded favorably to Spanish efforts to woo him to their side. He initially both disliked and distrusted the United

---

59. Storm, "Up the Tennessee in 1790," 127.
60. Atkinson, *Splendid Land, Splendid People*, 145.
61. McGillivray to Carondelet, November 1792, in Caughey, *McGillivray of the Creeks*, 345.
62. Calloway, *The American Revolution in Indian Country*, 238.
63. Ibid.

Southwest Territory Governor William Blount, considered to be one of the early founders of Tennessee, was a friend of Piominko and the Chickasaws. *By Washington B. Cooper, circa 1828-1884*

States and compared its efforts to court Native American allies to those of a cunning predator seeking its prey. He described it as "the cunning of the Rattle snake who caresses the Squirrel he intends to devour."[64] On his return from visiting the Louisiana governor in 1790 in New Orleans, two Americans whom Wolf's Friend met en route persuaded him to go to Cumberland. He accepted the offer to determine firsthand if Piominko had recently ceded any lands to the settlers there. Southwest Territory Governor William Blount received him at Cumberland. Having received nice gifts from his Spanish hosts in New Orleans, Wolf's Friend expected the same from Blount. The territorial governor did not disappoint and gave him a beautiful coat, which he readily accepted, and a hat. Finding the hat too small, he took it but planned to give it to his son as a wedding gift for his upcoming marriage. Sensing an opportunity to persuade Wolf's Friend to cede land to build a post at Ocochappo (Bear Creek), Blount pressed the question. Wolf's Friend immediately refused, saying he had the "Spaniards for his Whites; [and] that they furnished his nation with all the goods they wanted." Blount then looked at him "with evil eyes" and accused him of selling Chickasaw lands to the Spanish, something which Wolf's Friend quickly denied, saying, "they had no need of them." Worried, Blount asked him which side he would take if a war broke out between America and Spain. Wolf's Friend artfully told him neither, he would remain neutral "and stand back and let them fight one another."[65] As the hereditary civil minko of the Chickasaws with the majority of followers at that time, Wolf's Friend boasted that he could command Piominko to visit the Louisiana governor, saying, "I will send him Piomingo, who has Never given his Hand to the Spaniards, that I have to only Open my Mouth, and he will Obey, because he Is one of my Warriors."[66] Perhaps that would have been true years earlier, when civil minkos in Chickasaw society had more influence than war minkos, and when Piominko was younger. However, it was no longer the case, and Wolf's Friend greatly overestimated his control over Piominko and his growing influence.

Events in the fall of 1791 afforded Piominko an opportunity to demonstrate his friendship to James Robertson, his loyalty to the United States, and to punish enemies like the Shawnees, Kickapoos, and others. These tribal groups had loosely aligned in a western confederacy to stop American encroachment and to protect their lands northwest of the Ohio River. Robertson, now a gen-

---

64. Quoted in Charles A. Weeks, *Paths to a Middle Ground: The Diplomacy of Natchez, Boukfouka, Nogales, and San Fernando de las Barrancas, 1791-1795* (Tuscaloosa: University of Alabama Press, 2005), 141.

65. Copy of the Relation of Ugulayacabe of the Occurrences of his Journey to Cumberland, *American State Papers: Foreign Relations* 1: 281.

66. Quoted in Calloway, *The American Revolution in Indian Country*, 239.

eral, reached out to Piominko and his supporters on behalf of the United States to ask them to join in a campaign to strike some of these tribes who had also wreaked havoc in the Cumberland Valley. Piominko accepted the opportunity, knowing it served a two-fold purpose: weakening tribes that had threatened his community in the past and currying additional favor from his American counterparts for the weapons and support needed in a war with the Creeks.

Piominko and nineteen Chickasaw warriors left from Robertson's home on Richland Creek near Nashville and headed north to join American General Arthur St. Clair's forces near Fort Washington in present-day Cincinnati, Ohio. Robertson remained behind to watch over affairs at the growing Nashville settlement.[67] Piominko planned to proceed on to Philadelphia to visit Congress following the campaign.[68]

Piominko's quickly organized Chickasaw war party joined St. Clair's significant military force on October 27, 1791, just days before the campaign started. St. Clair, who was not feeling well when they arrived, briefly welcomed the war party and assigned its members to the First Regiment. Two days later, he sent Piominko's detail on a scouting patrol to outlying areas to capture any enemy warriors they encountered and to gather intelligence information. St. Clair assigned Captain Richard Sparks, an adopted Shawnee, and "four good riflemen" to accompany them on their mission. The group didn't plan to return for ten days unless they captured prisoners.[69] St. Clair's officers dressed them in distinctive handkerchiefs with a colorful plume to be worn around their heads so they wouldn't become victims of friendly fire when the battle started. He may have ensured they were on the reconnaissance mission when the fighting began for the same reason. If true, it suggests how much Washington and St. Clair valued Piominko as an ally and underscores that they could ill afford to lose him over mistaken identity.[70] While on patrol, Piominko's unit killed eight enemy soldiers, but it was to no avail.[71] St. Clair's poorly trained and poorly supplied, undisciplined, underfed, and ill forces proved no match for the well-orchestrated attack led by Little Turtle of the Miamis and Blue Jacket of the Shawnees. On November 4, 1791, the confederated tribes routed St. Clair's military in only a few hours and left hundreds of American soldiers

---

67. Putnam, *History of Middle Tennessee*, 363. Putnam reports the numbers as forty to fifty warriors, but all accounts, including St. Clair's papers and military diaries of participants, suggest it was twenty.

68. Winthrop Sargent, *Diary of Col. Winthrop Sargent: During the Campaign of MDCCXCI* (Georgia: Wormsloe, 1851), 21.

69. "St. Clair to Knox, 1 November 1791," and "The Campaign in Indian Country," in *The St. Clair Papers, Vol. II*, ed. William Henry Smith (Cincinnati: Robert Clarke & Co., 1882), 250, 256.

70. Atkinson, *Splendid Land, Splendid People*, 149.

71. Reprint of an undated letter from Charles Scott to Brigadier General James Wilkinson, *Scioto Gazette* (Chilicotte, Ohio), Vol. 1, Issue 20, 1.

LITTLE TURTLE.

Miami Chief Little Turtle led the Northern tribes during the North-west Indian War against American and allied Indian forces, which in-cluded Chickasaw warriors. His greatest victory was the defeat of General Arthur St. Clair's forces on November 4, 1791, a campaign that became known as St. Clair's Defeat, or the Battle of the Wabash. *Artist unknown*

Many held Major General Arthur St. Clair responsible for what was considered America's greatest military defeat at the time, the failed campaign against the Old Northwest tribes that later became known as St. Clair's Defeat, or the Battle of the Wabash. The Chickasaw warriors that fought with St. Clair were so disappointed in his command and military structure that American officials had to assure them he would no longer command troops in order to get them to agree to continue their military support. *By Charles Willson Peale, 1782, courtesy of Independence National Historical Park, Philadelphia*

and civilians dead. Little Turtle and Blue Jacket inflicted the largest defeat ever of the US Army to that point.

Weeks after the battle, Virginia Governor Lee Henry expressed grave concern to Washington that Piominko and his party had not been account-ed for. He feared perhaps they had perished in an ambush following the at-tack, without knowing the fate or disposition of St. Clair's army. In a letter to Washington, he attempted to console the president by offering his guarded optimism that against long odds Piominko survived. "The character of the Indian chief [Piominko] inspires me with hope," he wrote, "that he will elude the efforts of his enemy." Henry's wishes proved correct, but US officials had not yet received all the St. Clair reports. Fortunately, Piominko's detachment returned days after the massacre was over and likely witnessed the horrible carnage on the battlefield. Minko William Colbert (Chooshemataha) led a sec-ond Chickasaw party of warriors who had planned to rendezvous with Pio-minko's group and also join St. Clair's forces. He didn't arrive in time for the major battle, but instead helped with the retreat of St. Clair's survivors. An unnamed Chickasaw warrior distinguished himself as a hero during the bat-tle, as recorded in some of the newspapers covering the massacre and in Gov-ernor Henry's letter to President Washington. Eyewitnesses said he killed and scalped eleven enemies in hand-to-hand combat and died killing the twelfth.[72] While the records fail to name him, undoubtedly when he didn't return home from the battlefield, his Chickasaw community knew of his heroism, as his family celebrated his bravery while mourning his loss. Three years later, Gen-eral Anthony Wayne avenged St. Clair's defeat (also known as the Battle of the Wabash) and defeated the Old Northwest tribes at the Battle of Fallen Timbers. Once Piominko returned home from the disaster in Ohio, Blount wasted lit-tle time in contacting him and apologizing for the defeat and the manner in which St. Clair treated him. He promised him that the President would make it up to him with medals, clothing, money, rifles, and a personal gift of "three pounds of vermilion" from the governor, promises they soon kept. He hoped these tokens of appreciation would encourage Piominko to participate in fu-ture campaigns despite everything that went wrong in the last one.[73]

Newly appointed Natchez Governor Manuel Gayoso de Lemos convened a conference May 11, 1792, near his home to promote a post at Nogales, about ninety miles to the north. Located on a high bluff near the confluence of the

---

72. "To George Washington from Henry Lee, 4 December 1791," *Founders Online*, Na-tional Archives, last modified December 28, 2016, http://founders.archives.gov/documents /Washington/05-09-02-0150. [Original source: *The Papers of George Washington*, Presidential Series, vol. 9, *23 September 1791–29 February 1792*, ed. Mark A. Mastromarino. Charlottesville: University Press of Virginia, 2000, pp. 249–251.]

73. William Blount to Piamingo, the Great Chief and Warrior of the Chickasaws, 1792, *American State Papers: Indian Affairs* 1: 266.

BRIG? GEN. ANTHONY WAYNE.

Major General Anthony Wayne replaced Arthur St. Clair as commander of the American and allied Indian forces, which included Chickasaws, during the Northwest Indian War. He led his forces to victory
over the Northern tribes at the Battle of Fallen Timbers, resulting in
the end of the war and the signing of the Treaty of Greenville. *By Trum-
bull and Forest, courtesy of U.S. Library of Congress's National Digital
Library Program*

Yazoo and Mississippi Rivers in an area in present-day Vicksburg, Mississippi, the proposed fort represented a chess move to thwart American expansion and control of the Mississippi River. Initially Choctaw chiefs Franchimastabe, Taboca, Itelegana, and Chickasaw leadership sought to block the post since they had not consented to it. Well over two hundred attended the gathering, including large numbers of Choctaws and a Chickasaw delegation led by Taski Etoka. Neither Piominko or Wolf's Friend attended. After decades of often being on the opposite side of European alliances, the Choctaws and Chickasaws had resolved those differences. Spending five days together in activities, including two days playing stickball after they signed the treaty, they bonded well. During the opening of the negotiations on the morning of the eleventh under a large tent in Gayoso's garden, Gayoso and his staff sat in a half circle with Franchimastabe, and Taski Etoka sat in an armchair directly in front of them. Flanking them on either side were other leaders and warriors sitting on benches. The Choctaw and Chickasaw families who accompanied them remained at a campsite about three miles away and did not attend the negotiations. Pledging his commitment to previous agreements, Gayoso reassured conference attendees that the Spanish planned to honor trade regulations, resolve land disputes, and ensure the steady flow of trade goods to their communities. In exchange, he wanted the land to build the fort. Gayoso plied Taski Etoka with a variety of gifts including corn, brandy, eight rifles, five saddles, ammunition, nine barrels of gun powder, a hundred pesos, and the "keys to the Spanish storehouse" to pick out items he wanted. He also asked for and received a large Spanish medal. While the Choctaw leadership also received a variety of items, they remained divided over ceding the land for the post.[74] Gayoso's efforts paid dividends as in the end both Taski Etoka and the Choctaw representatives conceded the land for the fort in the Treaty of Natchez that concluded the meetings on the fourteenth. In short, the treaty provided Spain with the edge it desired to control traffic on the Mississippi River.

The following October, with the newly erected fort finished, Spain summoned the Creeks, Choctaws, Chickasaws, and Cherokees to create a southern alliance there. Well over a thousand participants joined the gathering, including Wolf's Friend and six other pro-Spanish Chickasaw leaders. The resulting 1793 Treaty of Nogales committed the four nations to an "offensive-defensive alliance." In return, Spain promised to provide the four tribes with protection, annual gifts, and commissioners to serve as liaisons. Piominko skipped the meeting. Noting his absence, Gayoso informed Louisiana Governor Carondelet that Piominko prevented them from having the full Chickasaw support and

---

74. "Manuel Gayoso de Lemos to Baron de Carondelet, Natchez, 29 May 1792," and "Treaty of Natchez, 14 May 1792," in Weeks, *Paths to the Middle Ground*, 184-202.

that he caused division as "a single chief who strays from the thinking of the rest." Gayoso proposed trying to persuade him to meet privately to win him to "their side."[75] Piominko never met secretly with him or other Spanish officials. Instead, he focused on negating the Natchez and Nogales agreements.

In August of 1792, Blount decided to follow up on his earlier meeting with Wolf's Friend and his reassurances to Piominko following St. Clair's defeat by convening a two-day conference with Chickasaw and Choctaw leadership in Nashville to clarify boundaries established in the Hopewell treaty. In particular, he wanted to focus on the land designated to build a post on Ocochappo (Bear Creek). Piominko, Wolf's Friend, and a large contingent of Chickasaw minkos participated. Juan Delavillebeuvre, Spanish commissioner to the Chickasaws and Choctaws, noted that 550 Chickasaws and 107 Choctaws attended the conference. Taski Etoka refused to go and visited a Creek village on the Tallapoosa River instead.[76] He sent his brother Chinnubby (also spelled Chinubbee, or Chimabi', "He Killed For You") in his place. Having never visited Nashville, Wolf's Friend called it a fitting place, as it represented to him the halfway point between nations where both had "warriors." He reiterated his position that he opposed the proposed post and quietly told both Chickasaw and Choctaw representatives that "Americans had hard shoes," and if permitted to build the post, "would tread upon their toes." Calling Americans his friends, Wolf's Friend asked that they not mention land negotiations in future discussions. As Piominko sat close to him waiting to address the conference participants, Wolf's Friend recognized him calling him a great warrior under him and stated all Piominko's previous agreements were binding to the Chickasaw Nation as whole.[77]

After Wolf's Friend finished, Piominko rose to speak, addressing the Chickasaw delegates at length first and then Blount and the other American officials. Holding his recent letter from Washington in one hand and the map he had drawn at Hopewell in the other, he reassured all gathered that peace remained preserved between the nations. Once he finished his opening remarks he got right to his point. "This map is old," he said, "I want a new one." His statement had nothing to do with the condition of the map in his hand, but rather the important boundaries it represented. Using the rivers as markers, he described in great detail the boundaries of the Chickasaw Nation. He reminded all those present that he drew the map he held in his hand "to save

---

75. "Gayoso to Carondelet, Natchez, 6 December 1793," and "Treaty of Nogales, 28 October 1793," in Weeks, *Paths to the Middle Ground*, 209-232.

76. "Delavillebeuvre to Carondelet, 12 September 1792" and "Delavillebeuvre to Gayoso, 10 September 1792" in *Spain in the Mississippi Valley, 1765-94, Vol. IV*, ed. Lawrence Kinnaird (Washington: U.S. Government Printing Office, 1946), 80-81.

77. Governor Blount to the Head-men of the Chiefs of the Chickasaws and Choctaws, 7 August 1792, American State Papers: Indian Affairs 1: 285.

his land" and he made it "plain" with uncomplicated boundaries. He worried if the boundaries were not clear it would lead to future conflict because of "the fondness of the Cherokees to sell land." He made it clear, however, that by distinctly drawing the boundaries on the map he did not mean to exclude the Cherokees and others from hunting on it as they had always done, but only meant to "preserve" Chickasaw land. He simply made sure that since the Cherokees didn't own the land they couldn't sell it. Piominko then asked Blount to take a copy of the map with the drawn boundaries to his uncle Little Turkey of the Cherokee Nation and explain their willingness to permit Cherokees to hunt in Chickasaw boundaries. Convinced that would prevent future bloodshed and resolve any disputes over the lands in question, Piominko said, "he will be pleased." In an emphatic statement he summed up his longstanding position on ceding lands: "I have made endeavors to preserve the land, and have ever refused to part with it." Piominko also reiterated that since the treaty at Hopewell he had reconsidered his position because times had changed, and he did not want a post built at Ocochappo (Bear Creek), fearing it would cause unnecessary loss of lives resulting from wars with the Creek and Cherokee Nations. When he finished speaking, Blount handed him a new map as Piominko had requested, but informed him that the treaty at Hopewell was still binding. Blount assured him that President Washington at least for the time being would honor his request to delay construction of the post.[78]

Saying he also spoke on behalf of Taski Etoka, Wolf's Friend said that he was in full agreement with Piominko's comments and all three "were appointed to do the business" of the Chickasaw Nation. Pleased with the conference discussions, Wolf's Friend offered a strand of white beads as a token of his hopes for peace and friendship and remarked "our children will be raised up in all happiness." Saying that Piominko convinced him to come to the meeting, he said "Piamingo and I are one; he is my father." Turning to Wolf's Friend, Blount remarked "that they [were] truly sensible of the great service that Piamingo has done his nation and the United States, and there is no doubt that he will lead his nation to happiness and glory, if they will continue to follow him." Blount closed by saying that President Washington wished to meet with a select few tribal leaders the following year in Philadelphia, and those invited would receive invitations. Closing the conference, the tribal groups came forward to receive gifts for attending. The "inhabitants of Long Town [Chokka' Falaa'] first marched up, with Piamingo at their head; and after, the other towns, according to their order, headed by their chiefs; and after the Chickasaws, the Choctaws according to their order." At the conclusion of the ceremony, Blount presented President Washington's promised medals and oth-

78. Ibid., 286-87.

Piominko marking map boundary lines at the Nashville conference. Though this interpretation places the scene indoors, the Nashville conference actually took place outdoors. *Sketch by James Blackburn*

er items to Piominko, William and George Colbert, and others for their valued service during the failed St. Clair campaign. Choctaw Chief Tloupoue Nantla also received one.[79] Secretary Knox, who facilitated the delivery of the articles, described both their purpose and appearance:

> The President of the United States is very desirous to reward the attachment of Piamingo, and the warriors who were with him at fort Washington, and he now sends to Piamingo, and two other principal chiefs [William and George Colbert], great silver medals, and each a suit of rich uniform clothes.[80]

The peace and friendship medals were handmade by New England silversmiths. The silver oval medals of 1792 came in three sizes – small, medium, and large – and roughly ranged from between 3 ⅜ inches to 6 ¾ inches in height and from 2 ⅜ inches to 5 inches in width. The front of the medal depicted George Washington smoking a peace pipe with a Native American, and the reverse had the presidential seal with an eagle holding thirteen arrows in its talons. US officials generally awarded the largest medal to the most important chief or minko, which often created jealousy among the other recipients.[81] The controversy surrounding which medal Piominko received will be addressed in the next chapter. Aside from the medals, Piominko and the Colberts each received a rifle, several woolen blankets, clothing, gunpowder, and other items. While the three Chickasaw leaders were the only ones to receive rifles, the warriors that accompanied them on the St. Clair campaign each received a half portion of the other items.[82]

When he sent the medals, Henry Knox personally promised Piominko that if his followers participated in future campaigns he would ensure they were well armed, well fed, and rewarded for their service with their choice of goods or money. He then extended an invitation from the president for Piominko and three other minkos to visit him soon in Philadelphia to demonstrate the "strong affections of the United States to the Chickasaw Nation" and extend wishes for their happiness.[83]

At Piominko's request at the conclusion of the Nashville meeting,

---

79. Delavillebeuvre to Carondelet, 12 September 1792, in Kinnaird, *Spain in the Mississippi Valley*, 83.

80. Knox to Chickasaw Nation, 17 February 1792, American State Papers: Indian Affairs 1: 249.

81. Robert Pickering, ed., *Peace Medals: Negotiating Power in Early America* (Tulsa, OK: Gilcrease Museum, 2011), 49-59.

82. Governor Blount to the Head-men of the Chiefs of the Chickasaws and Choctaws, 7 August 1792, American State Papers: Indian Affairs 1: 287-88.

83. Knox to Chickasaw Nation, 17 February 1792, American State Papers: Indian Affairs 1: 249.

Blount's aide presented the governor with a strand of white beads to forward to President Washington as a gesture, as Piominko put it, that "he will commence his journey early next spring" to meet him in Philadelphia. Spanish commissioner Delavillebeuvre noted in a letter to Louisiana Governor Carondelet that Blount designated four Chickasaw minkos, Piominko, Wolf's Friend, Chinnubby, and Mougoulachaminko (Imoklaasha' Minko'), whom Washington planned to entertain in the President's House in the nation's temporary capital.[84] Taking notice of the Nashville conference, McGillivray hoped to soothe Carondelet's potential concerns about the planned meeting in Philadelphia by falsely telling him that the Chickasaw and Choctaw chiefs and warriors that had gathered had no influence in their nations.[85]

Taski Etoka chose not to attend the Nashville conference, so he could instead focus on brokering better relations between the Creeks and Chickasaws. He hoped to orchestrate a meeting between Piominko and McGillivray, which the latter expected as well. By December 1792, McGillivray anticipated the upcoming meeting with Piominko, Wolf's Friend, and two others. He claimed that:

> Chickasaw mingo [Piominko] misbehaved himself to the point of threatening me with his going to the Americans, quitting my table, and leaving my house in vexation because I would not permit Turnbull to open a store for Indian trade at Yazou. I opposed it firmly. Nevertheless we are very good friends, since he received from me a Great Medal, certainly a masterpiece in work and size among the Indians.[86]

McGillivray may have temporarily blocked John Turnbull's post, but within three months Turnbull established one on the lower Yazoo River on Choctaw land. Shortly thereafter he established a second trading post further upriver near Chickasaw Bluffs with the blessing of the Chickasaws.[87]

Turnbull, a known trader, was married to a Chickasaw woman and also had the support of Carondelet. Panton, not wanting competition, opposed the post.[88] McGillivray probably initially tried to block the post to protect his friend Panton's interests. McGillivray offers the only account that he sent Piominko a medal. He also exaggerated and overstated the relationship between the two, and it is exceptionally unlikely, even for a short time, the two

---

84. Delavillebeuvre to Carondelet, 12 September 1792, in Kinnaird, *Spain in the Mississippi Valley*, 81.

85. McGillivray to Carondelet, 3 September 1792, in Caughey, *McGillivray of the Creeks*, 336.

86. McGillivray to Carondelet, 15 January 1793, in Caughey, *McGillivray of the Creeks*, 350.

87. Atkinson, *Splendid Land, Splendid People*, 289n25.

88. Weeks, *Paths to the Middle Ground*, 131.

were chummy. By January 1793, exasperated by their inability to persuade Piominko to join forces, McGillivray encouraged Governor Carondelet to stop reaching out to him. In writing to him, he said:

> I am to well acquainted with the Stubborn disposition of [Piominko] to believe that he will break his american Connexion by which his Vanity is gratifyd in being the leader & head of a [nation]& the Americans will retain him in their Interest [at any] expence.[89]

The proposed meeting between Piominko and McGillivray never occurred, as the latter died a month after writing the letter to the governor and before the peace arrangements had been finalized. Following the death of McGillivray, in early summer 1793, Choctaw middlemen delivered Creek peace belts to Piominko at Chokka' Falaa'. He reluctantly accepted the belts, but maintained that the Creeks were marauders and murderers.[90] As the storm clouds continued to gather, the path towards war between the two nations accelerated.

---

89. McGillivray to Carondelet, 15 January 1793, in Caughey, *McGillivray of the Creeks*, 351.
90. Calloway, *The American Revolution in Indian Country*, 240.

CHAPTER FOUR

GREAT BLAZE OF FIRE

———•◦•———

"We are now standing in the middle of a great blaze of fire,"

~ Piominko and other Chickasaw leaders, February 13, 1793, in a letter to General James Robertson regarding the pending war with the Creeks

———•◦•———

AFTER months of teetering on the brink of full-scale war, open fighting between the Creeks and Chickasaws erupted almost overnight. Passing within fifteen miles of Chickasaw villages on February 8, 1793, a band of Creek warriors surprised and attacked four Chickasaw warriors who were out on a hunt, killing one of them. They scalped him, mutilated his body, and threw him into a pond. Intending for the depredations to provoke and insult Piominko and the Chickasaws, the Creeks accomplished their purpose. Piominko had patiently avoided retaliating against earlier attacks, including the one that caused the death of his brother and nephew, but he could no longer restrain himself. His rage boiled over at the news of the attack. The time for waiting was over, and no one could persuade him otherwise. While others deliberated on the next step, Piominko dispatched Tatholah, a trusted associate, and forty warriors to search for the Creek war party.[1] Ironically, McGillivray, who spent months provoking Piominko, did not live long enough to see the Creek-Chickasaw war. He died in Pensacola just ten days after the attack on the Chickasaw hunters.

Chickasaw leadership immediately held a national council meeting at

---

1. Blount to Knox, 23 March 1793, American State Papers: Indian Affairs 1: 441.

Chokka' Falaa' and unanimously agreed to a declaration of war against the Creeks. Coincidently, three Cherokee leaders had recently arrived at the Chickasaw villages when news of the attack broke. They brought with them Natchez District Governor Gayoso's hopes to convince Chickasaw leaders to ally with Spain in its planned confederacy with other Southeastern tribes, and ironically and now implausibly to make peace with the Creeks. In particular, Gayoso had found a receptive diplomat in Cherokee Chief Bloody Fellow (Ne-netooyah), who he hoped could patch up differences between Piominko and Taski Etoka, and between the Chickasaws and Creeks. Bloody Fellow, however, found meeting with Taski Etoka futile as he suggested he drank excessively.[2] Gayoso encouraged him to instead meet privately with Piominko "to win him to the side of reason and to re-establish the King of that Nation in all his power."[3] Joining Bloody Fellow, Cherokee chiefs Bold Hunter (Toowayelloh) and John Taylor had decided to visit Piominko at his home village of Chokka' Falaa' on a return trip from meeting Spanish officials in New Orleans. As they departed the Louisiana city, Gayoso asked them to take a letter from Louisiana Governor Carondelet to Piominko and Wolf's Friend and to encourage them to come see him.[4]

The timing of their visit couldn't have been worse. They arrived at Chokka' Falaa' amid heightened tensions. Dismayed by the turn of events, the Cherokee leaders watched the council deliberations and tried to calm nerves, persuade, threaten, and in the end prevent Piominko and other Chickasaw leaders from making what the Cherokees considered a regrettable knee-jerk reaction. Entertaining none of their reasoning, Piominko angrily challenged them, saying he,

> desired them to desist; that he was so determined on war,
> that his very breath was bloody; that they might go home,
> and join the Creeks, if they chose it, as he supposed they
> would, for he knew they had long been at war with his
> friends, the people of the United States, though they pre-
> tended peace and friendship.[5]

His harsh words likely stung the Cherokee visitors, whom Piominko undoubt-edly knew well from his time growing up in their villages. All of them were close associates of his uncle Little Turkey, who was now one of the leading headmen of the Cherokees. Bloody Fellow quickly sent a letter to Governor

2. A.P. Whitaker, "Spain and the Cherokee Indians, 1783-98," *The North Carolina Historical Review* 4, no. 3 (1927): 260.

3. Quoted in Charles A. Weeks, *Paths to a Middle Ground: The Diplomacy of Natchez, Boukfouka, Nogales, and San Fernando de las Barrancas, 1791-1795* (Tuscaloosa: University of Alabama Press, 2005), 98.

4. Ibid.

5. Ibid.

Francisco Luis Hector, baron de Carondelet was the Spanish governor of Louisiana and West Florida from 1791 to 1797. He extended many overtures to the Chickasaws in an effort to win their support for Spain. Although he was never able to influence Piominko, his efforts did temporarily gain favor with other Chickasaw leaders, most notably Chickasaw Minko Wolf's Friend. *By Alberto Junquera, courtesy of Louisiana State Museum*

Carondelet explaining the tense situation. The Creeks started the conflict, he said, and by spilling Chickasaw blood and killing the "warrior of Piomingo" they now ruined any hope for fulfilling the Cherokee's mission to foster diplomacy. Bloody Fellow promised to try to reason with Piominko, calling him an "old friend" and Cherokee speaker.[6] Bloody Fellow delivered the letter from Carondelet to Piominko, which expressed Carondelet's hope that the warring Creeks and Chickasaws could find a peaceful resolution to their disagreements and invited Piominko to visit him. Piominko and the other Chickasaw leaders immediately formed a respectful, but firm, reply to the governor. They informed him of the murder of the Chickasaw hunter and suggested that Spain also bore some responsibility for it and other Creek hostilities by providing them with weapons and ammunition. He promised immediate revenge against the Creeks.[7]

At nearly the same time, Piominko quickly penned a letter to his close friend General James Robertson reminding him of America's obligations to rally to their defense as they sought retribution against the Creeks. In it he said,

> although we wish to be at peace with all, the Creeks have spilt our blood, and we desire you will despatch expresses to every head-man in America, particularly to General Washington, the Secretary of War, Governor Blount, and the head-men at Kentucky, on fort Washington, and General Pickens, to let them know that our agreement was to be as one man, in regard to our enemies and friends; that, if one was struck, the other was to feel the blow, and be one cause.[8]

Piominko then expressed hope Washington or Robertson would send warriors to join the Chickasaw, "to let the Creeks know what war is." He closed his fervent letter by also requesting muskets, rifles, flint smoothbores, ten blunderbusses, six swivel guns and a weapons expert to help operate them, gunsmiths, and tools. He also needed corn and food supplies because a famine had besieged the Chickasaws. Requesting that aid come immediately, he said, "we are now standing in the middle of a great blaze of fire."[9] Piominko then departed for Chickasaw Bluffs with representatives from each of the three largest Chickasaw villages on an undertaking to personally ask American officials for ten cannons.[10]

---

6. Weeks, *Paths to the Middle Ground*, 99; James Atkinson, *Splendid Land, Splendid People: The Chickasaw Indians to Removal* (Tuscaloosa: University of Alabama Press, 2004), 155.

7. Atkinson, *Splendid Land, Splendid People*, 155.

8. "The Chickasaw Chiefs to General Robertson, 13 February 1793," American State Papers: Indian Affairs 1: 442.

9. Ibid.

10. Atkinson, *Splendid Land, Splendid People*, 156.

Spanish officials later determined the unfortunate incident with the Chickasaw hunter resulted from a perceived Creek need for blood revenge. Nearly six months prior to the murder of the Chickasaw hunter, one Creek warrior had killed another so he could steal his rifle. When he returned to his village, he blamed the death on Chickasaw warriors. Seeking vengeance, the relatives of the murdered Creek killed the first Chickasaw they encountered.[11]

Shortly thereafter, a small band of Creek warriors stopped at the house of trader Hardy Perry. Hearing the news that Creek warriors were there, Chickasaw warriors entered the house and killed three of them. Counted among the dead were the brother and nephew of Creek War Chief Mad Dog (also called Efau Hadjo). As an individual of nearly comparable rank to Piominko, Mad Dog's painful loss evened the score, avenging the loss of Piominko's brother and nephew at the hand of Creeks. However, that did not mean the fighting was over. In fact, it had barely started.[12] Mad Dog threatened retaliation in a letter to Creek Indian agent James Seagrove, writing, "we mean to have satisfaction, for, if they had killed them in the woods, we might try to make it up; but, killing them as they did, we cannot put up with it."[13] Days after the attack at Perry's house, deputy agent of Indian affairs Timothy Barnard warned Seagrove that two thousand well-organized Upper Creek warriors had departed for Chickasaw villages and threatened to destroy the nation.[14] Other sources place the number at closer to eight hundred. Led by McGillivray's brother in-law, the former French military officer Louis Le Clerc Milfort, they planned to force the Chickasaws to surrender and to take the women and children prisoner. If they surrendered unconditionally, Milfort instructed his men to kill only Piominko and his supporters.[15] However, the Creeks aborted their mission after they arrived at the Chickasaw communities. Some sources suggest they stopped on Spain's orders, while others argue they found the Chickasaw heavily fortified within "upwards of thirty forts" and abandoned a potentially futile attack.[16] It appears both assertions are correct. As the large force of Creeks approached the villages, one of William Panton's couriers delivered a letter to them from Arturo O'Neill, the Spanish governor of West Florida, asking them to turn around and seek peace instead. Had O'Neill not intervened, both

---

11. Atkinson, *Splendid Land, Splendid People*, 283n36; Weeks, *Paths to the Middle Ground*, 111.

12. Letter from Mad Dog, The White Lieutenant, David Cornell, Alexander Cornell, Mr Weathorford, and thirteen headmen of Upper Creeks, 8 April 1793, American State Papers: Indian Affairs 1: 384.

13. Ibid.

14. Timothy Barnard to James Seagrove, 19 April 1793, American State Papers: Indian Affairs 1: 387.

15. Atkinson, *Splendid Land, Splendid People*, 158-159.

16. General James Robertson to General Smith, 20 July 1793, American State Papers: Indian Affairs 1: 465.

sides would have undoubtedly taken heavy casualties, though the Creeks had a significant numerical advantage. As it turned out, Milfort's war party would have been thwarted in their attempts to target Piominko and his supporters, anyway, as he and a number of his warriors were away at Chickasaw Bluffs receiving a significant amount of much-needed corn sent by Robertson.[17]

As tensions with the Creeks intensified, the factionalized Chickasaws unified and rallied to prepare for an extensive war. Taski Etoka, Wolf's Friend, and other minkos urged the Choctaws to join their cause and cautioned Spain to not interfere in Chickasaw recruitment of Choctaw allies. They also pressed Spain to immediately cut off supplies and weapons to the Creeks. Wolf's Friend also had an intensely personal stake in the war, following the recent burning death of his nephew at the hands of Creek warriors, and he, too, demanded justice.[18]

Spain worked behind the scenes to end the hostilities between the two nations, worried that the United States would fill the void if they didn't. While remaining staunchly loyal to the Americans, Piominko entertained peace discussions with Spanish officials. Chickasaw and Choctaw leaders gathered on June 1, 1793, at Piominko's home in Chokka' Falaa' to explore options. In a lengthy address, Choctaw Chief Tuscoonopoy presented the Chickasaws with a wampum belt from the Creek Nation, intended as an olive branch to broker peace. The belt had been delivered by couriers from Spanish West Florida and William Panton following the Spanish orders that had stopped Milfort's large Creek war party from attacking the Chickasaw villages. Chickasaw leader Mucklesa Minko readily accepted the gift as a sign of the dawn of a new day. Mucklesa Minko passed the belt to Piominko, who clutched it with both hands. While Piominko hoped for peace, he knew a token of proposed armistice was no guarantee of it. In an eloquent oration, Piominko articulated both his frustrations, an overview of the Creek hostilities, and his hopes.

> My friends and relations headmen & Warriors of the Chickasaw Nation: You see me. I have now taken the peace string of Wampum fetched by the Creeks by our brothers the Chactaws: You see me now I have got it fast, seizing with both hands, declaring a peace on my part: I never wanted war with these people: I have put up with their insults for these six years past: In the first place they killed two of my town. I put up with it; since they have been stealing our horses, killing our white people & still I said nothing: and at last came to my Nation and killed one of

17. Atkinson, *Splendid Land, Splendid People*, 159.
18. Ibid., 156, 158.

our own people, which was sufficient to raise the blood of any man of spirit, but I still put up with it, as it was the talk of our Fathers the Spaniards to keep peace among the red people. After which they killed some of our Nation in their own land, which raised us in general for a War this is a bad situation: almost starved to death; no place of defence for our Women and children, but our brothers the Americans were good enough to send us a little corn to support life, and we have now built us Forts, & now they send a peace Talk. I have said [to] my Warriors that I never would make while I was alive without I get satisfaction, but since it is the talk of our younger Brothers and beloved friends the Chactaws for peace, our beloved headman Hylaycabby for peace who has lost his near Relation, and our Nation for peace in general, why should I stand out that is but one man? No! I take the talk and confirm it on my side, in case the Creeks do not break it: They have made very light of us as I have heard, saying that we were but a handful of people, they could lay us desolate in a little time. I look on them in as light a manner as they do me, for I don't think they are Warriors, they are thieves and Murderers, that is their chief calling for a living. But I take this peace talk hoping they will comply with it on their side for the future. And now my Warriors and Women and Children, let the dark cloud that has been over us for so long be blown off and the Sun shine clear on us, & each of you to your devotion or calling that you follow, and the Fruits that Nature sends prosper us so famished.[19]

He closed by promising to attend a meeting on the Yazoo River proposed by Governor Gayoso. Acknowledging the Spanish had unsuccessfully tried to meet with him multiple times, he said he bore them no ill will and commented, "I cannot imagine what they want to see me for," but if his nation wished, he would go. Most likely, he had a pretty good idea why Gayoso wanted to meet. "I will go the straight path to the Assembly," he reassured all present.[20]

While well-intentioned, Piominko's trail toward peace and a potential meeting with Gayoso was neither linear nor unobstructed. When it looked like Spain's proposed meeting might come to pass, Mad Dog and other Creek leaders pressed Spanish officials for assurances that Piominko would partici-

---

19. Indian Speeches Made at Long Town, 1 June 1793, in *Spain in the Mississippi Valley, 1765-94, Vol. IV*, ed. Lawrence Kinnaird (Washington: U.S. Government Printing Office, 1946), 165-166.
20. Ibid., 166-167.

pate. They argued they had more than enough issues they wanted to discuss with him. Sporadic hostilities between the two nations, however, continued to thwart any hopes for a lasting peace. Instead of meeting in person, Piominko penned a letter to the Creeks unabashedly placing the blame for the tensions squarely on them. Arguing that their forebearers once got along nicely, he maintained the new generation of Creek leaders was more interested in spilling blood than living in harmony. Criticizing them for saying one thing and doing another, he said they spoke as if they had "two tongues to speak with." He offered them advice, telling them if they wished to keep their land they should learn to get along with Native and non-Native neighbors. After planned meetings with the Spanish fell through, Piominko opted to seek munitions and food from his American allies. Spain countered his move by sending corn to the Chickasaws and continuing efforts to broker peace between the two nations it desperately courted.[21]

In early summer 1793, Piominko took time out from the Creek conflicts to attend the funeral of his friends and tribal members John Morris and his brother James Anderson. The latter had fought with Piominko in the St. Clair campaign. Both had been murdered about two hundred yards from Governor Blount's house in Knoxville. Authorities charged Jacob Clement, Daniel Sleekley, and three others with their deaths. The murders turned out to be the result of a horrible case of mistaken identity. Cherokee warriors had killed and scalped Clement's two sons, and he sought revenge. When Clement and his group attacked Morris and Anderson, they apparently thought the two brothers were Cherokees, and not Chickasaws, with whom they were friendly. Robertson had entertained John Morris in his home numerous times, and both brothers were beloved by the Knoxville community. Robertson authorized the burial of Morris in a non-Native cemetery in the city with military honors "due to a warrior of his friendly nation" (a likely reference to Piominko). Robertson walked in the large, military-led funeral procession with the Morris family, Piominko, and other Chickasaw representatives.[22]

Besides managing the war with the Creeks, Chickasaws also helped the Americans. In 1792, still reeling from St. Clair's defeat the year before, President Washington appointed General "Mad Anthony" Wayne to lead military operations in the Old Northwest. Wayne ordered construction of several forts in the area. Having learned from St. Clair's failures, he also drilled soldiers to ensure a well-trained and well-armed military. He used Robertson and Knox as mediators to reach out to Piominko and his warriors in early 1794 and asked

---

21. Weeks, *Paths to the Middle Ground*, 110-111, 114.

22. Robertson to Blount, 24 May 1793 and 28 May 1793, American State Papers: Indian Affairs 1: 454-455; "Gov. Blount's Order for His Burial," *Salem Gazette* (Salem, Massachusetts), July 16, 1793, Vol. VII, Issue 353, Page 2.

them to join his forces in a campaign against the same tribes they had fought with St. Clair near present-day Cincinnati. Not only did the opportunity afford the Chickasaws the chance to gain more weapons and favors, it also allowed them the chance to even the score against long-standing enemies like the Kickapoo. Yet Robertson cautioned Wayne that the Chickasaw Nation remained deeply divided over whether to ally with Spain or America, and as he expected, many of the villages refused to join Wayne's crusade. General Wayne sent weapons to Piominko's pro-American Chickasaw volunteers via Chickasaw Minko Jimmy Underwood and Lt. William Clark, of Lewis and Clark fame. Chickasaw and Choctaw warriors arrived at Robertson's home in Nashville in waves throughout April and May of 1794, where he outfitted them to join Wayne's army. The groups departed for the campaign at different times from April through late June. Piominko and some of his warriors left with a large group of Choctaws in mid-May. William Colbert led a separate group of about a hundred Chickasaw warriors and left at roughly the same time.

Neither Piominko nor Colbert's group were to join with Wayne. Piominko, George and Joseph Colbert, Muckleshamingo (Mucklesa Minko, or Imoklaasha' Minko'), and a small contingent of Chickasaws, separated from their party to travel to a planned meeting with President Washington in Philadelphia. Robertson intended to travel with his friend as far as Holston, Virginia, and Piominko hoped Robertson's son would accompany them to Philadelphia. Meanwhile, Colbert's group was en route to join Wayne in the north, but they received word in July of a second pending Creek attack on the Chickasaw villages, similar to the aborted one the year before, and turned back home to defend their homeland. The Creeks threatened to destroy the Chickasaws if they did not surrender Piominko, Wolf's Friend, William Colbert, and Major William Glover for execution for the death of Mad Dog's brother. When the Creek war party drew close to the Chickasaw villages they had a change of heart, perhaps realizing that Colbert and Piominko were away from the villages. Instead of seeking retribution, they sent five warriors forward carrying a banner of peace to seek a diplomatic solution.[23]

While Piominko traveled to Philadelphia and the Creeks threatened war, Blount and Robertson had gunmaker Thomas Simpson make a special rifle Piominko had requested in 1793. The highly ornate, handcrafted Pennsylvania Kentucky long rifle was the epitome of craftsmanship and certainly worthy of someone of Piominko's stature. Simpson may have modeled the rifle after one owned by legendary Tennessee long hunter Kasper (sometimes

23. John Haywood, *The Civil and Political History of the State of Tennessee: From its Earliest Settlement Up to the Year 1796* (Nashville, TN: Publishing house of the Methodist Episcopal church, South, 1891), 425; Atkinson, *Splendid Land, Splendid People*, 163-164, 286n10; Piamingo to General Robertson, 17 June 1793, American State Papers: Indian Affairs 1: 466.

spelled Gaspar) Mansker. In a letter to Robertson the year before, Piominko had requested Robertson "to get Simpson to make me a gun like Colonel Mansker's."[24] As mentioned in chapter 2, Piominko had spared the lives of Mansker and several other long hunters when they crossed paths on the Cumberland River near Nashville in 1770. Simpson billed the United States $53.39 for the rifle, which represented the high-end price of comparable rifles of the time. Likely it involved numerous carvings and would have taken Simpson well over a week to create. All of Simpson's handmade rifles came with a matching powder horn that mimicked the carvings on the gun. Within a year the breech on the rifle malfunctioned and Piominko requested its repair, which Blount arranged for a gunsmith to do and had it returned to him. Blount agreed to pay the repair costs.[25]

Piominko's Chickasaw entourage arrived on the outskirts of Philadelphia on June 29, 1794. They were met at the edge of the city by a small contingent of American officials that included Colonel Robert Hayes and Secretary of War Knox. When they drew within a mile of the heart of the city, companies of light cavalry and infantry escorted the entourage, and curious onlookers, to a Doherty's Tavern for a brief planned reception. Blount had appointed the strikingly red-headed and burly Captain John Chisholm to accompany the Chickasaws during their stay in the city. Chisholm had served Blount, Sevier, and others since their time together in the failed State of Franklin. Blount and Sevier frequently sent him on informal diplomatic missions to the Creeks, Choctaws, Cherokees, and Chickasaws. It is likely Piominko knew him well.[26]

Once they had rested from their long journey, Piominko and his cohorts met with President Washington at the President's House on Market Street in Philadelphia at noon on July 11, 1794. The first Congress established Philadelphia as a temporary capital while architects and laborers created the permanent capital in Washington, D.C. The stately three-story, redbrick President's House had been the home of financier Robert Morris. When guests entered the President's House, an entry with a nearly thirty-eight-foot ceiling and substantial and refined arched passageways led them to the state dining room

---

24. Piomingo to General Robertson, 17 June 1793, *American State Papers: Indian Affairs* 1: 466.

25. Mel Hankla, "Riflemen of the Cumberland and the Guns That Made Them Famous," *Kentucky Rifle Association Bulletin* 40, no. 3 (Spring 2014): 8-9; Blount to Colonel David Henley, 29 July 1795, at VolunteerVoices.Org (Tennessee Electronic Library), http://diglib.lib.utk.edu /cgi/t/text/pageviewer-idx?c=vvb;cc=vvb;rgn=full%20text;view=image;seq=0000000001; idno=0023_000059_000207_0000&q1=chickasaw&op2=And&q2=&op3=And&q3=&rgn= main.

26. "Piamingo, Chickasaw," *Knoxville Gazette*, July 31, 1794, Vol. 3, Issue 17, Page 3; "Winchester, July 7," *General Advertiser*, July 14, 1794, Page 3; Kate White, "John Chisholm, Soldier of Fortune," *Chronicles of Oklahoma* 8, no. 2, (June, 1930): 233-239, http://digital.library.okstate .edu/Chronicles/v008/v008p233.html.

In 1793 Piominko sent a letter to General James Robertson requesting American officials employ renowned gunsmith Thomas Simpson to make him a Kentucky long rifle similar to one Simpson had made for Colonel Kasper Mansker two years earlier. The top rifle pictured above is believed to be Mansker's 1791 Simpson rifle that Piominko's rifle was modeled after. *Courtesy of Tom Eblen/Lexington Herald-Leader*

Right:
*1926 President's House,
courtesy of PhillyHistory.org*

Below:
*President's House, courtesy
of National Park Service,
photo by Joseph E.B. Elliott*

The President's house in Philadelphia where Piominko and other Chickasaws met with President George Washington in 1794. The structure no longer exists, however, a temporary structure was created in 1926 for Philadelphia's sesquicentennial celebration and is pictured in the black and white photo above. A permanent interpretive structure, pictured in the color photo above, currently sits on the exact location of the original President's House. This structure is part of the Independence National Historical Park site.

where most formal receptions occurred. Recently renovated, the room featured a large elegant and dramatic two-story bow, which likely inspired the similar Blue Room at the White House.[27]

George Colbert, Muckleshamingo (Mucklesa Minko, or Imoklaasha' Minko'), possibly Minko William Glover, seven warriors, three of their sons, and interpreter Joseph Colbert accompanied Piominko and his son into the curved room where Washington greeted them. John Quincy Adams, and presumably Knox, joined the conclave. Secretary of the Treasury Alexander Hamilton had planned to attend the meeting, but his son was ill, preventing him from participating.[28] Adams kept a descriptive diary of the events that transpired in the room that day. The Chickasaw delegation arrived in a variety of dress, aptly described by Adams as ranging from,

> coarse jackets and trowsers, and some in the uniforms of the United States. Some of them had shirts, and some had none. There were none of them either painted or scarified, and there were four or five with rings through their noses. One or two had large plates, apparently of silver, hanging upon the breast, I do not recall observing any other ornaments upon them.[29]

Washington invited his guests to sit in a circle. Apparently trying to accommodate his Native American visitors, he then opened the meeting in a humorous and odd way.

> As soon as the whole were seated, the ceremony began. A large East Indian pipe was placed in the middle of the Hall. The tube, which appeared to be of leather, was twelve or fifteen feet in length. The President began, and after two or three whiffs, passed the tube to Piomingo; he to the next Chief and so all around. Whether this ceremony is really of Indian origin, as is generally supposed, I confess I have some doubt. At least these Indians appeared to be quite unused to it, and from the manner of going through it, looked as if they were submitting to a process in compliance to *our* custom. Some of them, I thought smiled with such an expression of countenance as denoted a sense of

27. Independence Hall Association, "The President's House in Philadelphia," http://www.ushistory.org/presidentshouse.

28. "From Alexander Hamilton to George Washington, [11 July 1794]," *Founders Online*, National Archives, last modified December 28, 2016, http://founders.archives.gov/documents/Hamilton/01-16-02-0590. [Original source: *The Papers of Alexander Hamilton*, vol. 16, *February 1794–July 1794*, ed. Harold C. Syrett. New York: Columbia University Press, 1972, p. 591.]

29. Charles Frances Adams, ed., *Memoirs of John Quincy Adams: Comprising Portions of His Diary, From 1795-1848, Vol. I* (Philadelphia: J.B. Lippencott & Co., 1874), 35-36.

novelty, and *frivolity* too; as if the ceremony struck them, not only as new, but as ridiculous.[30]

The somewhat comical ceremony ended, and Washington delivered remarks prepared by Knox. The president thanked "the great Spirit," for bringing them safely to Philadelphia where he had longed to meet them, and said, "I love the Chickasaws and it will always afford me sincere satisfaction, to be instrumental to their happiness in any way or manner." Remarking that their participation in the St. Clair campaign demonstrated the highest level of friendship between the two nations, he encouraged them to join the United States in an upcoming engagement with the same tribes. If they did so, he promised to cover their expenses and furnish them "Goods for your nation, your families and yourselves." He encouraged them to continue on to New York City, and if they did so, he would make the accommodations for their visit. He also promised free education for their sons. He closed, telling them to make themselves "at home and take comfort accordingly."[31] As the president finished each sentence, he paused for the interpreter to translate it. Listening intently to his words, Adams noted that the interpreter repeated to the five represented Chickasaw minkos the same word twice, "Tshkyer! Tshkyer!" after each translated sentence. Linguist John Dyson has suggested that the word Adams probably heard was actually *aacha'shki,* which means, "truly this is what is being said."[32] When Washington finished his speech, Piominko declined an invitation to speak, saying he didn't feel well. He promised to speak in a couple of days, which he did. He and the other Chickasaw leaders, however, probed the president about another recent meeting in the same President's House days earlier with a Cherokee delegation. Their careful questions represented "a mixture of curiosity and animosity," and they warned the president to tread carefully with the Cherokees. As Adams wrote, the Chickasaw spoke of them as "a perfidious people." The meeting lasted nearly an hour and concluded with an informal reception of wine, punch, and cake. While enjoying the light refreshments, Washington took one last opportunity to remind them "that the Chickasaws had always been distinguished as sincere, and faithful friends, and that the United States has always valued such friends most highly." They quietly accepted his comments, but didn't acknowledge the compliment.[33]

Piominko and the Chickasaw delegation met at least once more, on July 21, with Knox while in Philadelphia. There is no indication Washington attend-

---

30. Ibid., 34-35.

31. Secretary of War to the President, 11 July 1794, and Draft of a Speech to the Chickasaw Indians, 11 July 1794, in *The Territorial Papers of the United States, Vol. IV,* ed. Clarence Edwin Carter (Washington: United States Printing Office, 1936), 349-350.

32. Richard Green, *Chickasaw Lives Volume Three: Sketches Past and Present* (Ada, OK: Chickasaw Press, 2010), 42.

33. Adams, *Memoirs of John Quincy Adams,* 35.

ed the meeting. Knox presented Piominko with a document, signed by Knox and the president, which set the same boundaries for the Chickasaw Nation as agreed upon at the 1792 Nashville conference.[34] The instrument also protected Chickasaw lands and in effect gave them unrestricted title to it. Following the July 21 meeting, Knox requested that large peace medals and silver arm bands and wrist bands be delivered to the Chickasaws, along with numerous smaller medals, broaches, nose jewels, and ear bobs of varying sizes. He also sent 150 rifles as gifts.[35]

Washington further ensured that Piominko and his party knew before they left town that he valued their alliance and unwavering loyalty to him and the new republic by having Knox deliver to them an additional assortment of clothing and other gifts for each member of the party, their families, and others who had remained behind in the Chickasaw Nation. Knox made arrangements to have the items transported to Knoxville, to be picked up there by Piominko and the others on the journey home. In addition, Piominko received six hundred pesos, coins widely circulated in America at the time, and each member of his delegation received thirty pesos to spend in the stores as they pleased. President Washington also promised the Chickasaw Nation a three-thousand-dollar annuity and issued a commission to Wolf's Friend, who was unable to attend the meetings. Congress ratified the annuity payments through two separate acts and paid them until 1903. While Piominko's party appreciated the gifts, some expressed disappointment they did not receive vermilion, a coveted natural red dye. When the shipment arrived nearly five months later, Washington had added some items to it, hoping to offset the apparent dismay over the unavailability of the brightly colored pigment.[36]

Within weeks of the historic meeting between the Chickasaws and President Washington, General Wayne's forces mobilized for an assault on the Shawnee- and Miami-led confederacy in present-day Ohio. Culminating in the Battle of Fallen Timbers, Wayne dealt the Ohio Valley tribes a decisive blow that led to the Treaty of Greenville the following year. Though Piominko had planned at one point to join Wayne, it doesn't appear he did, despite a widely read contemporary newspaper reporting that he arrived and commanded over a hundred warriors.[37] The paper erroneously placed his arrival in Ohio to join Wayne at the same time he was meeting with Washington in Philadelphia. No other accounts or official records note his participation in the well-known bat-

---

34. Haywood, *The Civil and Political History of the State of Tennessee*, 425.

35. Henry Knox to Samuel Hodgdon, 21 July 1794, and Knox to General Edward Hand, 25, July 1794, at *Papers of the War Department, 1784-1800*, Center for History and New Media, http://wardepartmentpapers.org.

36. Haywood, *The Civil and Political History of the State of Tennessee*, 427; Atkinson, *Splendid Land, Splendid People*, 165-167.

37. "Piomingo, Mountain Leader," *Independent Gazetteer*, July 9, 1794, Page 3.

Piominko and other Chickasaw leaders and warriors met with President George Washington at the President's House in Philadelphia in 1794. *Sketch by James Blackburn*

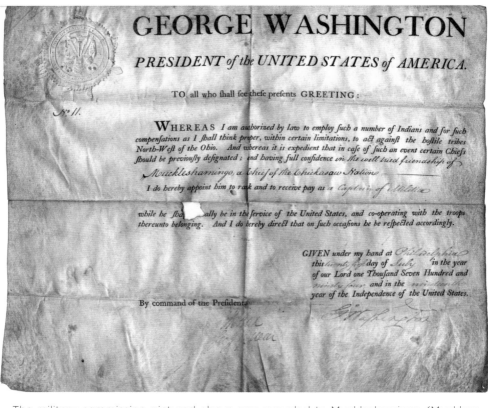

GEORGE WASHINGTON

PRESIDENT of the UNITED STATES of AMERICA.

TO all who shall see these presents GREETING:

Nᵒ. 11.

WHEREAS I am authorized by law to employ such a number of Indians and for such compensations as I shall think proper, within certain limitations, to act against the hostile tribes North-West of the Ohio. And whereas it is expedient that in case of such an event certain Chiefs should be previously designated; and having full confidence in the well tried friendship of *Muckleshamingo, a Chief of the Chickasaw Nation* I do hereby appoint him to rank and to receive pay as *a Captain of Militia* while he shall actually be in the service of the United States, and co-operating with the troops thereunto belonging. And I do hereby direct that on such occasions he be respected accordingly.

GIVEN under my hand at *Philadelphia* this *twenty fifth* day of *July* in the year of our Lord one Thousand Seven Hundred and *ninety four* and in the *nineteenth* year of the Independence of the United States.

By command of the President

G. Washington

The military commission pictured above was awarded to Muckleshamingo (Mucklesa Minko, or Imoklaasha' Minko') by President George Washington in 1794. Muckleshamingo was likely one of the five Chickasaw leaders recorded by John Quincy Adams as accompanying Piominko to the meeting with Washington at the President's House on July 11, 1794. Thus, this commission is likely very similar to the one Piominko received during that visit. Today the commission is housed at the Oklahoma Historical Society in Oklahoma City, Oklahoma. *Courtesy of the Oklahoma Historical Society; Minor Collection 1985.044. Washington, George (Commission) issued By President Washington To Muckleshamingo Naming Him Captain Of The Militia*

tle, and it is highly doubtful they would have not recorded it. While Piominko and most, if not all, of his party did not take part in Wayne's campaign, some Chickasaws did, serving as invaluable scouts. Shortly after the Battle of Fallen Timbers and before Piominko returned to Chokka' Falaa' from his meeting with Washington, Chickasaw Minko Taski Etoka died. His brother Chinnubby replaced him and continued to ally with Spain.[38]

It is unclear when Piominko's entourage arrived home from Philadelphia, but he received the goods promised in the meetings with Washington and Knox on November 3 in Knoxville. Delivered weeks earlier at Chickasaw Bluffs on a boat appropriately named *Opoiamingo*, the goods were then transported by carriers on horses a few hundred miles east to waiting Chickasaw representatives. *Opoiamingo's* captain, John Gordon, had instructions to sell the boat at Chickasaw Bluffs for the best price to recover some of the expenses related to the goods and their delivery. Six small howitzers with several rounds of ammunition were also onboard, likely ordered by Knox the previous May to aid the Chickasaws against Creek attacks. With a temporary lull in hostilities between the Creeks and Chickasaws, Knox apparently feared the cannons would disrupt the fragile peace and sent rushed orders to stop delivery of the weapons, probably diverting them to Nashville.[39] Shortly after receiving the goods, Piominko and his group left Knoxville to deliver them to the Chickasaw Homeland.

Within a few days of his departure from Knoxville, rumors circulated that he and his group had been killed by a band of Cherokee warriors. The false information was quickly spread by the Creeks, though it is unclear whether they were aware the story was untrue. When Piominko failed to show up at a designated spot on the Ocochappo (Bear Creek) on the southwest bank of the Tennessee River, Chickasaw anxieties about the rumors reached fever pitch, and animosity toward the Cherokee quickly rose. While William, George, and Levi Colbert waited with a large group for Piominko's uncertain arrival, news spread of a Cherokee party in six canoes passing nearby on the Tennessee River. William and George Colbert decided to split their men into two parties and station themselves on either side of the river to ambush and destroy the approaching Cherokee travelers in retaliation for Piominko's presumed murder. Fortunately, after a lengthy and vigorous debate, Levi persuaded his brothers to let the canoes pass safely until they had solid information on Piominko's fate.[40]

Levi's judgment proved right. He and a companion then traveled to

---

38. Atkinson, *Splendid Land, Splendid People*, 167-169.
39. Ibid., 166-167.
40. Robertson to Blount, 7 November 1794, and McCleish to Blount, 7 November 1794, American State Papers: Indian Affairs 1: 539-540.

This monument near Maumee, Ohio commemorates the Battle of Fallen Timbers in which American troops and allied Indian forces, including Chickasaw warriors, led by General Anthony Wayne defeated Northern tribes ending the Northwest Indian War. *Photo by Doug Kerr, CC 2.0, flickr.com*

Nashville to look for the missing leader. To his relief, Piominko arrived there safely on November 7. The convoy that his brothers nearly attacked on the Tennessee River turned out to be peaceful Cherokee families attempting to escape the horrific violence in the region, and they would have been victims of a horrible misunderstanding.

While Levi was in Nashville seeking information on Piominko, his brother William's rash behavior proved unfortunate for another Cherokee family traveling on the river, a distance behind the larger and earlier fleet. When William tried to flag them down they fled out of fear, and he assumed that action implied their guilt in the death of Piominko. He forced them ashore and they ran into the woods where they were captured. He killed and scalped the man and took two women and two children as prisoners. Several Chickasaws, fearing repercussions, thought it best to transport the captives to Nashville. When Chickasaw John McCleish (McClish) informed Robertson of the identity of the man Colbert killed, both kept it secret, likely to prevent Cherokee retaliation. The efforts to not take the prisoners to one of the Chickasaw villages as trophies of war and the secrecy surrounding keeping their identities quiet suggest the Cherokee family held some status. In a letter to Blount detailing the incident, Robertson wrote that William Colbert had warned if the Cherokee sought vengeance he would "cry havoc! and let loose the dog of war" on them and accuse them of starting the conflict. When Piominko received word of William Colbert's action, he had Levi deliver a message to Chickasaws at Muscle Shoals, telling them to gather there and wait patiently for him to arrive. Presumably, he wanted an emergency meeting to address the pending crisis and prevent it from escalating further.[41] Robertson and McCleish's secret wasn't as hush-hush as they hoped, for the Cherokees and Creeks already knew. A passing Cherokee party on the Tennessee River sighted a Chickasaw camp with a Cherokee canoe on the shore riddled with musket ball holes. Near the abandoned canoe they saw a Cherokee woman gathering water by the river bank who had been taken prisoner by the Chickasaws. Similarly, a Creek party traveling through the highly trafficked area witnessed the same scene and debated attacking the Chickasaw camp to liberate the captive, but determined they didn't have enough warriors.[42]

Fortunately, no Cherokee attacks occurred as a result of the death of the Cherokee traveler and the capture of his family. The Cherokees vastly outnumbered the Chickasaws, and while retaliation would have proven costly to both sides, the Chickasaw villages would have paid a heavy price. Levi Colbert's instincts to let the Cherokee fleet of canoes pass saved many lives, while

41. Ibid.
42. Blount to Robertson, 22 January 1795, in "Correspondence of General James Robertson," *The American Historical Magazine* 4, no. 2 (April 1899): 168.

107

his brother William's rashness could have cost many more. It is probable that when Piominko returned to Muscle Shoals he diplomatically resolved the disagreement with his prominent Cherokee uncle, Little Turkey. Little Turkey sent Piominko's son with a message from the principal chief of the Cherokee Nation to Piominko asking for fair restitution. Little Turkey well understood that Piominko's son was one of the few individuals who could safely travel from Cherokee villages to the heart of the Chickasaw Nation. "We don't want to spoil or make the Path Bloody," Little Turkey stated. "We would [be] glad to make peace with them."[43] Apparently uncle and nephew reached a diplomatic solution, as war did not result from the tensions.

While the Chickasaws narrowly averted a war with the Cherokee, they were unable to do so with their old nemesis the Creek Nation. Events that had been building for years finally came to head as the fragile and temporary peace suddenly broke. On January 2, 1795, nearly two months after the events surrounding the erroneous reports of Piominko's demise at Cherokee hands, William Colbert and a large party of Chickasaw warriors including Captain James Underwood, Captain Mucklishapoy the elder, and the Old Counselor, discovered a small Creek camp along the Duck River in middle Tennessee. Colbert's warriors attacked the camp at daybreak and killed and scalped five Creeks. The dead included Shotlatoke and his brother, who Chickasaw leaders maintained had committed numerous depredations against them over the years. Pleased with the scalps they took, Colbert's group of nearly a hundred arrived at Robertson's house a few days later. Not only did the Chickasaws believe they had rid their territory of thorns in their side, but also adversaries of American settlers in the area. Robertson expressed his satisfaction to them that the group had been killed, but also his concern that the attack would trigger a full-scale war. Colbert's group vigorously pressed Robertson to build blockhouses on Chickasaw land where a well-traveled road intersected the Tennessee River at a site called the "Creek crossing point."

They volunteered to help with construction and hoped it would serve as an American and Chickasaw defensive fortification and as a place from which to launch military strikes during an anticipated spring war with the Creeks. Having recently received a commission from President Washington, Colbert vowed to remain in the Nashville area with his large force to defend the region until his proposed fort could be built. Demonstrating his resolve, his Creek wife, children, and six slaves accompanied him to plant crops and establish temporary residency. Governor Blount sent Colbert's request to the president. Nearly two months later, Timothy Pickering, the new secretary of war, said

---

43. Little Turkey to Robertson, 10 April 1795, in "Correspondence of General James Robertson," *The American Historical Magazine* 4, no. 3 (July 1899): 248-249.

that Washington approved of the post at the proposed Chickasaw site, but only for purposes of trade for all the tribes in the region. He also cautioned that at the Nashville conference in 1792 Piominko vehemently refused the construction of any posts in that location.[44]

While Colbert campaigned for an American post on the Tennessee River, Spain secretly lobbied Wolf's Friend for one at Chickasaw Bluffs on the Mississippi River in present-day Memphis. While waiting for the anticipated authorization from Wolf's Friend and his supporters, Governor Gayoso picked a prime spot and claimed it for Spain. Within days Spanish soldiers cleared the lot and started construction of the fort. Gayoso named it Fort San Fernando de las Barrancas for Spain's crown prince and future king, Ferdinand VII. Nearly two weeks after Spain occupied the site, a forty-member Chickasaw delegation arrived with messages from Wolf's Friend and Chinnubby, who apparently granted approval for the new post. On June 20, Chickasaw minkos William Glover and Payehuma, Gayoso, and several others signed a treaty ceding the Chickasaw land for the post to the Spanish. Gayoso signaled the signing of the important document with a multiple cannon and artillery salute. Over the next two months Wolf's Friend and Chinnubby visited the fort at separate times, accompanied by their families and large numbers of Chickasaws. Piominko remained conspicuously absent. In addition to the customary gifts offered as part of treaty exchanges, Spain authorized annual payments of five hundred pesos to Wolf's Friend for his faithfulness. The first payment was received during negotiations for the Chickasaw Bluffs land, and payments continued until 1802. Spain's financial incentives appear to have served their purpose, as Wolf's Friend quickly acquiesced to the post's construction in a place that Piominko had long contested. The new Spanish post, albeit short-lived, provided a trading house for Panton, Leslie and Company and an armed garrison for one hundred fifty Spanish soldiers.[45]

Nearly two weeks after Colbert's attack on Shotlatoke's party, Blount predicted in a letter to Robertson that the Creeks would not respond for months. He argued it would take time for the news to filter back to the Creek Nation and a large, deliberate, and measured military response would take months to orchestrate.[46] In the interim, Colbert's party struck again in early March 1795 when they surprised and pursued a party of Creek warriors, killing

---

44. Robertson to Blount, 13 January 1795, in "Correspondence of General James Robertson," *The American Historical Magazine* 4, no. 2 (April 1899): 163-165; Blount to Robertson, 20 January 1795, Ibid.: 165-167; Timothy Pickering to Robertson, 23 March 1795, Ibid.: 182-186.

45. Arrell Gibson, *The Chickasaws* (Norman: University of Oklahoma Press, 1971), 88-89; Atkinson, *Splendid Land, Splendid People*, 171-172.

46. Blount to Robertson, 20 January 1795, in "Correspondence of General James Robertson," *The American Historical Magazine* 4, no. 2 (April 1899): 166.

This map shows the plan for the Spanish fort that would eventually be named Fort San Fernando de las Barrancas, near the junction of the River Margot (Wolf River) and the Mississippi River at Chickasaw Bluffs, in present-day Memphis, Tennessee. Spain withdrew from the area in 1795 and destroyed the fort. *Courtesy of David Rumsey Map Collection, davidrumsey.com*

ten and taking six prisoners.[47] Blount's prediction proved correct. The Creeks attacked Chokka' Falaa' in May and again in September of 1795, hoping to kill Piominko and his allies and decimate his village. After word spread in late spring of the impending attack on Chokka' Falaa', Robertson and Blount dispatched two parties of Cumberland volunteers, totaling nearly a hundred men, to help defend the Chickasaw village. One party, led by Captain David Smith and William Colbert, traveled overland, and the other party, commanded by Colonel Kasper Mansker and Captain John Gwyn, went by boat. Both groups arrived within ten days of each other and well ahead of the Creek advance. They joined Piominko's village behind its well-armed and fortified stockades.

When the Creek party, variously estimated from three hundred to a thousand warriors, approached the village in May, the Chokka' Falaa' residents at first mistook them for reinforcements from Wolf's Friend's Chisha' Talla'a' community. An alert Chickasaw sentinel who spoke Creek asked their tribal affiliation as they approached and quickly realized their identity. When the frontline of Creek warriors arrived, they encountered two women and a man outside the stockade gathering wood. They killed and scalped them. Positioned behind a four-pound cannon in the stockade, Mansker witnessed the brutal attack and sought to take his soldiers outside the barricades to pursue those who murdered them. The cannon Mansker manned is likely the one Robertson had sent the Chickasaws, and which Carondelet had complained to Robertson about in 1793, saying, "which although is a small caliber, is a dangerous weapon in the possession of savages."[48]

Colbert initially refused Mansker's request to pursue the murderers. He believed the Creek advance team represented a decoy to draw them into a larger ambush, which would then storm the stockade killing the women and children inside. However, outraged relatives of the slain individuals left the stockade, seeking retribution. Colbert and his men charged outside to protect them and caught the Creeks completely off guard, killing or wounding several of them. Facing a village better fortified than they expected, with a cannon and support from Cumberland volunteers, and surprised by Colbert's spontaneous counterattack, the Creek party abandoned their attack and retreated towards home. Several days later, the Cumberland settlers also returned to their homes in the Nashville area. In the interim period between attacks, Blount sent Robertson to Chokka' Falaa' to see Piominko, hoping to broker a peace agreement between the warring nations. In particular, Robertson sought the return of several Creeks the Chickasaws had taken prisoner. These were probably the prisoners Colbert captured in his March raid. The Chickasaws agreed to re-

47. "Indian News," *Kentucky Gazette*, March 28, 1795, Page 2.
48. Carondelet to Robertson, 21 May 1793, in *The Spanish Regime in Missouri, Vol. II*, ed. Louis Houck (Chicago: Donnelly & Sons, 1909), 21.

lease the captives if the Creeks demonstrated a desire for permanent peace.[49] Out of respect for Robertson, Creek chiefs prohibited any attacks on Piominko during his visit. That peace, however, proved short-lived after Robertson left.[50]

Largely unsuccessful in their May assault, the Creeks orchestrated a much larger one in September. At the time of the September attack William Colbert was away from the villages, meeting with President Washington in Philadelphia to seek weapons, ammunition, and a new title. Feeling the trip unnecessary and unwarranted, Robertson tried to discourage him from going. While in Philadelphia, Colbert privately lobbied the president to openly recognize him as the favored war leader over Piominko. Washington refused, however, and denied further military assistance to the Chickasaws in their conflict with the Creeks. In order to appease Colbert, the commander in chief awarded him the title of major.[51]

As a drizzling September rain fell, about a thousand warriors marched again on Piominko's village. Many were on horseback, and they brought plenty of ammunition, clothing, blankets, and drums, expecting after a long siege to capture and occupy Chokka' Falaa'. Piominko later recounted to Robertson that the Creeks camped for the night near Colbert's fort, just west of the main part of the town. Early in the morning they launched their assault in a bow-shaped line that stretched a half mile in length and killed a Chickasaw woman outside the fortress. Feeling poorly, George Colbert rallied the Chokka' Falaa' warriors in defense of the village. They waited in ambush alongside their Chokkilissa' counterparts while the Creek contingent drew closer. Although Colbert's horse was shot from under him during the fighting, the trap worked to perfection. Catching the Creek force completely off guard, the Chickasaws routed them and pursued them for five miles, attacking their rear guard and flank. In their haste to retreat, the disarrayed Creek warriors abandoned their supplies. That probably saved their lives, as many of the Chickasaw warriors stopped chasing them to collect the war spoils and take it back to their villages. George Stiggins, son of an English trader and Creek mother, fought on the Creek side in the attack. His version of events closely matches that of Piominko. He recalled the Creeks attacking William Colbert's fort first, and then being surprised by Chickasaw warriors rushing its defense, which caused them to panic, turn, and flee. Stiggins maintained the mounted Creek war chiefs tried desperately to stop the retreat and press the attack, but to no avail.

49. "Knoxville, October 2," *The City Gazette* (Charleston), November 11, 1795, Page 2.

50. A.W. Putnam, *History of Middle Tennessee: Or, Life and Times of General James Robertson* (Nashville: Tennessee Historical Society, 1859), 519-520, 526; Haywood, *The Civil and Political History of the State of Tennessee*, 449-450, 457, 460-61; James R. Atkinson, "A Narrative Based on an Interview with Malcolm McGee by Lyman C. Draper," *Journal of Mississippi History* 66 (Spring 2004): 51; Atkinson, *Splendid Land, Splendid People*, 174-175.

51. Putnam, *History of Middle Tennessee*, 526; Atkinson, *Splendid Land, Splendid People*, 175-176.

Although outnumbered "fifty to one," he recalled, the Chickasaw defenders repelled them, and he thought they killed and wounded larger numbers of Creeks than even Piominko suggested.[52]

Though at least twenty-six Creeks died and as many were wounded, it could have been far worse. According to Piominko, "six warriors and a woman" lost their lives, including his son-in-law and a distinguished minko named Underwood.[53] While the quick retreat may have spared Creek lives, it cost some of them their dignity. Robertson wrote to Colonel David Henley that several of them received "well-deserved" floggings when they returned home without their belongings.[54] Interpreter Malcom McGee noted that after the attack Piominko was blamed for remaining behind in the center of the town with a four-pound cannon while the important battle raged.[55] No records have been found to date that explain his actions. He doesn't mention it in his letter to Robertson. Perhaps he was ill, or thought that location was the best place to station the howitzer to defend the elderly, women, and children or, since he was one of the primary targets of the attack, that was considered the best place to keep him secure. It is doubtful that fear overcame him. Throughout his life he never shied from battle or risks to himself, and as a result few ever questioned his courage or whether he deserved his elevated status as a warrior. While the feuding nations fought sporadically over the next two years, the second battle at Chokka' Falaa' largely represented the end of the Creek and Chickasaw wars and the beginning of lasting peace between the two nations.[56] Fortunately, Piominko had survived numerous Creek attempts on his life. As one historian put it, "he had been hunted as a partridge on the mountains."[57]

Following the September 1795 attack at Chokka' Falaa' both the Creeks

52. Opy Omingo to Robertson, 29 September 1795, at *Tennessee: A Documentary History*, The University of Tennessee Libraries, http://diglib.lib.utk.edu/cgi/t/text/text-idx?c=tdh; cc=tdh;sid=62fd0108c329fd5a7c9168d09bcd01cc;q1=Chickasaw%20Indians--Government %20relations;rgn=main;view=text;idno=tl023; George Stiggins, *Creek Indian History: A Historical Narrative of the Genealogy, Traditions, and Downfall of the Ispocoga or Creek Indian Tribe of Indians*, ed. Virginia Pounds Brown (Birmingham: University of Alabama Press, 1989), 75-76.

53. Opy Omingo to Robertson, 29 September 1795, at *Tennessee: A Documentary History*, The University of Tennessee Libraries. (See note 51).

54. Robertson to Henley, 24 October 1795, at *Tennessee: A Documentary History*, The University of Tennessee Libraries, http://diglib.lib.utk.edu/cgi/t/text/text-idx?c=tdh;cc=tdh;sid= 62fd0108c329fd5a7c9168d09bcd01cc;q1=Chickasaw%20Indians--Government%20 relations;rgn=main;view=text;idno=tl023.

55. Atkinson, *Splendid Land, Splendid People*, 177.

56. Opy Omingo to Robertson, 29 September 1795, at *Tennessee: A Documentary History*, The University of Tennessee Libraries. (See note 51); *Philadelphia Aurora General Advertiser*, November 30, 1795, Issue 1542, Page 2; Gibson, *The Chickasaws*, 89-90; Putnam, *History of Middle Tennessee*, 526-527; Atkinson, "A Narrative Based on an Interview with Malcolm McGee," 52; Haywood, *The Civil and Political History of the State of Tennessee*, 460-465.

57. Putnam, *History of Middle Tennessee*, 508.

and Chickasaws agreed to a truce. As part of the agreement each nation agreed to accompany the other to Philadelphia to see Secretary of War James McHenry and permanently settle their differences.[58] Piominko, George Colbert, and four other Chickasaw leaders made the trip to Philadelphia in 1796.[59] Delegates from the Choctaw and Cherokee nations also went along to air their grievances and resolve boundary disputes. The culturally similar traveling companions of Southeastern tribes were sometimes friendly towards each other, and other times were bitter enemies. Captain John Chisholm escorted them to the arranged meeting.

Piominko, Colbert, and the others arrived in Philadelphia on December 2. Once there, US officials arranged a tour for them at the Peale Museum, named after artist and naturalist Charles Willson Peale. Created a decade earlier and before the Smithsonian was established, the museum represented America's premier natural history repository at the time. A group of tribal leaders from the Old Northwest tribes were also invited to tour the museum that day. Leaders from the Shawnee, Miami, Ojibwa, Pottawatomi, and other northern tribes had met with President Washington three days earlier at the President's House, where he addressed them and gave them gifts. Whether officials scheduled the tours to overlap purposely is unclear, but none of the groups had agreed to planned meetings together. While rounding one of the corridors on the first floor of the Philosophical Hall of the museum, Shawnee leaders Blue Jacket, Red Pole, and the rest of the Old Northwest tribes' coterie accidentally ran into Piominko, Colbert, and the Southeastern tribes' contingent. Just a few years earlier, members of the two parties had been adversaries during St. Clair's and Wayne's campaigns. Had they crossed paths in the Ohio valley or Cumberland region under different circumstances the outcome may have been different, but the museum provided the right setting to encourage a more peaceful encounter.

As the groups found themselves face-to-face surrounded by the exhibits, their warriors instinctively went for their knives, preparing for confrontation. Fortunately, interpreter William Wells was traveling with the Old Northwest group and reacted quickly to diffuse the situation. Wells knew Piominko, and likely some of the other leaders with him. He and the two other interpreters with him, calmed them and negotiated an unexpected and spontaneous peace conference the following day in a room provided by the museum.[60]

---

58. Blount to Robertson, 11 April 1796, in "Correspondence of General James Robertson," *The American Historical Magazine* 4, no. 3 (July 1899): 280.

59. John B. M'Ferrin, D.D., *History of Methodism in Tennessee: From the Year 1783 to 1804, Vol. 1* (Nashville, TN: Publishing House of the M.E. Church, 1888), 308.

60. William Heath, *William Wells and the Struggle for the Old Northwest* (Norman: University of Oklahoma Press, 2015), 237-238.

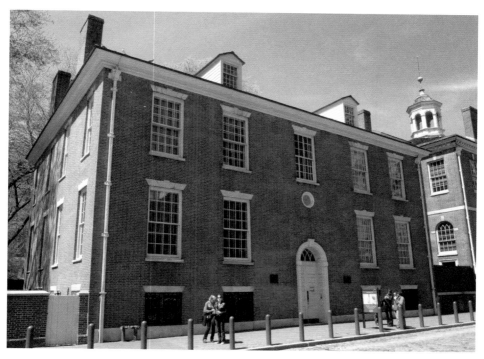

In 1796 Piominko and George Colbert toured the Peale Museum located in this Philadelphia building, which today is home to the American Philosophical Society. During the
tour, Piominko and Colbert ran into leaders from the Northern tribes they had fought
against with the Americans during the Northwest Indian War. The situation could have
ignited a deadly altercation. Instead, cooler heads prevailed and peace talks effectively
ended any residual hostilities. *Courtesy of American Philosophical Society, Philosophical
Hall, photo by Brent Wahl*

Wells had been captured by Miami warriors as an adolescent and was adopted by a Miami chief who raised him as his son. He later married one of Miami War Chief Little Turtle's daughters. After fighting with the Miamis against St. Clair, Wells had a change of heart and joined Wayne's forces as a scout and interpreter. He served as an interpreter at the Treaty of Greenville following Wayne's victory at the Battle of Fallen Timbers, and the United States paid him handsomely over the next couple of years for his services. It was General Wayne that had assigned Wells to accompany the Old Northwest chiefs to Philadelphia to meet with the president.[61]

Four days after the fortuitous meeting at the Peale Museum, the *Philadelphia Gazette* reported on the incident:

> An accident of so extraordinary and interesting nature occurred on Friday last, as it justifies its relation, without incurring a rigid responsibility for the minute circumstances stated. There are now in the city Indians to the number of about fifty from the tribes all of Choctaws, Chickasaws, Cherokees, upper and lower Creeks. Nearly an equal number of each of these tribes visited Peale's Museum on the same morning within a few minutes of each other. They at first occupied different parts of the room; and seemed surprised at the site of each other. They manifested some degree of jealousy and indisposition to associate together. No two tribes, it is said, understood the same language. The obstacles to a friendly intercourse were gradually removed, and the Chiefs of the different tribes cautiously approached each other. A conversation soon ensued by means of the interpreters. The Secretary of War was requested to attend, and he was soon followed by the President of the United States, who in a short address, recommended to them peace and harmony among themselves. The Chiefs are stated to have exhibited marked signs of pleasure; and after a free communication of sentiment, they withdrew to a private room, and entered into an alliance of peace, which was definitively concluded with every sign of sincerity and solemnity.[62]

McHenry and Washington jumped at the unexpected opportunity to put the complications of all the recent conflicts behind them. With the trib-

---

61. Paul A. Hutton, "William Wells: Frontier Scout and Indian Agent," *Indiana Magazine of History* 74, no. 3: 183-222, https://scholarworks.iu.edu/journals/index.php/imh/article/view/10110/13931.

62. *Philadelphia Gazette*, December 6, 1796, Vol. XIII, Issue 2533, Page 2, Fourth Column.

al delegates in the museum, outside of the comforts of their home nations, the peace discussions had a chance to bear fruit. Secretary of War McHenry opened the peace talks, saying,

> The president of the United States, your Father who loves you as his Children, has heard the request which some of you have made to him and agreed that you should all meet in one Assembly to strengthen before me, as a solemn Witnesses, that Chain of Friendship which ought to connect you together, and which he wishes may continue like the Sun, always bright. The Great Spirit whom your Father the President and the People of the United States above, requires from Men of every color and language that they should live in peace and love each other. Nations which engage in War and forsake this part are sure to be hurt, though they should kill a great many of those they fight against; for war is a fire that burns the large Trees as well as the small ones. To avoid this trouble five good Chiefs and wise Men, whenever a dispute or difference happens between the people of their respective Nations will meet and try to have it settled, in a peaceable manner, and rather than go to War, will give up something to which they think they have a right.[63]

When he finished, representatives from several of the nations spoke, articulately expressing their desire to put past differences behind them, and then exchanged strings of beads of friendship. In an important symbolic gesture, the Creek delegation stood and shook hands with McHenry, Piominko, and George Colbert. Meyaneta, a Chickasaw minko, then delivered expressive and well-spoken remarks:

> I am now going to speak to the Cherokees and northern Indians as they have passed the Talks between our Nation and the Creeks. The Red People are here met together by the desire of their elder Brothers, the Whites; I advised them therefore to attend to and remember this Talk – that are the Cherokees, Creeks, Choctaws, Chickasaws and the Northern Indians present. I am glad to stand up on my feet and deliver you this Talk and I am greatly pleased that you are all here to hear it – I desire that all the sharp weapons of war may be thrown away – be lost in [illegible],

---

63. Speech to the Indians from the Secretary at War, Urging Peace into the Future, and Replies, 2 December 1796, at *Papers of the War Department, 1784 to 1800*, Center for History and New Media, http://wardepartmentpapers.org.

> And never again found – Let us consider that we are all
> Red People and ought ever to remain in peace with each
> other – The Sun shines bright – for my part, although I
> see my skin appears to be red – yet I cannot help think-
> ing that it is white – I have listened to the good Talks – I
> have now done; there is no use in long Talks – all of you
> have heard what I have said – and I hold this Talk with my
> five fingers.[64]

Near the end of the long meeting, the Shawnee chief Red Pole (also called Mes-
quakinoe) expressed his desire that the discussions adjourn to get something
to eat. Sensing progress and an opportunity to put all grievances on the table,
Piominko rose and declined Red Pole's petition to recess, saying he wished to
remain longer. Piominko closed the meeting with his remarks:

> The Red People have all finished their Talks – I hope they
> will remember them when they are at home – and if any of
> their Blood is spilt, to enquire into the reason before they
> strike – by that means peace will be preserved – if any of
> the Red People should meet with any damage – let them
> find out the persons who did it and ask for satisfaction be-
> fore they attempt to talk it – I do not speak to the Red Peo-
> ple – I include the Whites also – the Country is over-run
> with them, and they will be apt, by their encroachments
> to do mischief. This is all I have to say.[65]

Tragically Red Pole, despite the care of multiple doctors, died of pneumonia on his way home from the conference, and they buried him in the Trin-
ity Cathedral churchyard in Pittsburgh. At the recommendation of Major Isaac
Craig, commandant at Fort Pitt, McHenry authorized the headstone placed
over his grave with the inscription "Lamented by the United the States."[66]
Within months of his death, the Peale Museum created wax figures in his
likeness and that of Blue Jacket, out of respect for their contributions at the
peace conference.[67]

When the highly productive, accidental peace conference ended, the
Chickasaw delegates remained in the city to press McHenry on their original
purpose for traveling there. They wanted him to destroy the recently vacated
Spanish fort at Chickasaw Bluffs and assure them America did not intend to

---

64. Ibid.

65. Ibid.

66. "Death of Red Pole," and Isaac Craig to James McHenry, 2 February 1797, at *Papers of the War Department, 1784 to 1800*, Center for History and New Media, http://wardepartmentpapers .org.

67. "Additions to Peale's Museum," *Claypoole's American Daily Advertiser*, August 12, 1797, Issue 5725, Page 3.

build a garrison in its place. They also wanted to address potential American encroachment within Chickasaw boundaries.[68] In October of 1795, a month after the last Creek attack on Chokka' Falaa', Spain suddenly pulled out of the Mississippi valley. Signing the Treaty of San Lorenzo (Pinckney's Treaty) that year, Spain opened the Mississippi River to American navigation and abandoned their positions north of the thirty-first parallel. When Piominko visited Philadelphia two months after the signing of the treaty, he expressed particular concern about the future of Fort San Fernando de las Barrancas.

After multiple delays, Spain finally abandoned the fort in 1797, destroying it as they departed. Within four months, American Captain Isaac Guion arrived at the site, and with William Colbert's permission, erected a US fort, named Fort Adams, after John Adams. The construction of the American fort reopened Chickasaw factional fissures. Colbert, Piominko, and Wolf's Friend arrived at the contested site at different times as tensions rose. On the opposite side of the river, a Spanish force of about a hundred soldiers under the command of Colonel Charles Howard who hadn't left despite Pinckney's Treaty, returned at the request of Wolf's Friend, hoping to retake the site. Displaying no signs of threatening actions, Howard afforded Guion proper respect and deference and kept a reasonable distance, waiting. While Guion distributed gifts in exchange for consent to build the post, Wolf's Friend demanded a meeting with Howard and everyone present to determine which country, if any, would occupy the location. After being scolded by Wolf's Friend several times for building the fort, the American captain set a meeting for October 16 so all interested parties could attend.

Piominko had visited the location in mid-August. Guion noted he arrived in "bad health," and he observed a noticeable "coolness" between the Mountain Leader and Wolf's Friend. Shortly thereafter, Piominko and William Colbert returned home to defend against an anticipated Creek attack that failed to occur. Guion set the mid-October meeting time so Piominko and Colbert could return to attend.[69]

Colbert opened the meeting and wasted little time in reproaching Wolf's Friend and Captain Howard, who begrudgingly attended at Wolf's Friend's request. Colbert looked directly at Wolf's Friend and forcefully told him,

> I know your object is to expel the Americans and bring
> back your friends the Spaniards. But this shall not be while
> I live. The works now being built here were begun with
> my consent. I and my people gave our consent and our

---

68. Chiefs of the Chickasaws to James McHenry, 15 December 1796, at *Papers of the War Department, 1784 to 1800*, Center for History and New Media, http://wardepartmentpapers.org.

69. A.R. James, *Standard History of Memphis, Tennessee: From a Study of the Original Sources* (Knoxville, TN: H. W. Crew, 1912), 47-49.

promise and I would like to see the man or the chief who can make that promise void. The Americans may go away if they choose to go. I hear you talk of force. You will do well to count the warriors of this nation. Before you can drive the Americans you must first kill me and my warriors and bury us here.[70]

Piominko then stood and delivered similar, strongly worded remarks. He sided with Colbert and didn't protest the construction of the new American post. Wolf's Friend sat "moody and silent." His long-held hopes of a Spanish partnership completely ended that day, and with it some of the influence and leverage he and his faction held. The United States finally had a fort in the strategic location along the Mississippi and near the rapidly growing Memphis that it had long coveted. Once completed, officials renamed the post Fort Pike because they wanted to use Adams' name on a larger post in Natchez, Mississippi. In 1801, Captain Zebulon Pike closed the fort that bore his name and relocated it two miles to the south on a higher part of the bluff overlooking the river. Following that move, it was renamed Fort Pickering for Washington's secretary of war, Timothy Pickering.[71] Piominko would not live to see Fort Pickering built.

When the door suddenly closed with the signing of Pinckney's Treaty, Spain's Chickasaw supporters like Wolf's Friend and his followers felt betrayed. Spain's withdrawal from the Mississippi valley signaled the end of one of the last imperial struggles to play out across the Chickasaw Homeland and the Southeast. The United States was now the last country standing and the Chickasaw Nation's only non-Native ally. Piominko's course of action proved to be the right one. From his operational bases in the Cumberland region and his home of Chokka' Falaa', he had pushed for the path of peace, friendship, and partnership with the United States. While the European chess game of playing one Native American community off the other during the last several decades of the eighteenth century had threatened to split the Chickasaw Nation in many parts, it failed. When the last Spanish post closed in the Mississippi valley and Spain withdrew, the Chickasaw Nation remained intact. In the end, Wolf's Friend, Piominko, Chinnubby, and others coalesced and placed Chickasaw needs, unity, independence, and sovereignty above all else. In particular, Wolf's Friend and Piominko quickly put aside any differences of opinion they may have once had, and after 1797 they were united in supporting the Americans.

Piominko never seemed to recover from the ill health Captain Guion made note of during discussions over the construction of the American fort at Chickasaw Bluffs. The records relating to him after this time largely go silent.

---

70. Ibid., 49.
71. Ibid., 50-51.

Sometime in 1799, probably surrounded by his wife and children on a ridge in his beloved Chokka' Falaa', the renowned leader passed away. He likely had not reached his fiftieth birthday. While we know nothing about his cause of death or the events leading up to his final journey on earth, we can assume that when word of his death spread throughout the Chickasaw villages, wailing from his loved ones and admirers filled the air as an immense sadness spread from town to town. He has had few equals in Chickasaw history.

Before Piominko was laid to rest, his loved ones likely anointed his hair with oil and painted his face red, as was their custom. They would have dressed him in his finest clothes and adorned him with beads, ornaments, and valued personal items. The Chickasaw custom was to bury him beneath his house, seated facing east.[72] Surely, his family and friends took comfort in the extraordinary life he led in his short time on earth.

In 1956, developer Luther Roberson unearthed a grave while excavating for street construction in a new housing addition in Tupelo, near the site of the former Chokka' Falaa' village. In a well-argued article, historian James Atkinson contends that the grave Roberson unintentionally discovered was Piominko's. In addition to skeletal remains the grave contained a saddle, a rifle, brass US officer's buttons, a gold epaulet, silver arm cuffs and other silver ornaments, and a Washington peace medal. Each matches an item known to have been owned by Piominko, and all certainly would have been appropriate for the burial of someone of Piominko's exceptionally high standing. The only other reasonable possibility, according to Atkinson, is that the grave was that of William Colbert, who died in 1824 and owned similar items, including a peace medal. However, Colbert's last known home and his probable burial spot, Atkinson claims, is miles from the grave Roberson uncovered. For those reasons, Atkinson concludes the grave is likely Piominko's.[73] Roberson displayed the objects at his home for several years, and today the collection remains in private hands.

In 1935, construction crews working on a highway, near Tupelo, Mississippi, unearthed a peace medal almost identical to the one found later by Roberson. Tupelo resident J.T. Ross spotted the medal the moment the road equipment unearthed it.[74] The Ross medal is on display at the Smithsonian Institution's National Portrait Gallery. While researching the two peace medals found in the Tupelo area, author Mitch Caver and Chickasaw archaeologist

---

72. John R. Swanton, "Social and Religious Beliefs and Usages of the Chickasaw Indians," *Forty-Fourth Annual Report of the Bureau of American Ethnology* (Washington, D.C.: Government Printing Office, 1928), 229-235.

73. James R. Atkinson, "Death of A Chickasaw Leader: Probable Grave of Piomingo," *Mississippi Archaeology* 35, no 2. (Winter 2000): 124-172.

74. *The Commercial Appeal* (Memphis) 1935.

1793 Washington peace medal from the Smithsonian National Portrait Gallery, Schermer Collection. This medal is also known as the Ross medal. It was found by Tupelo, Mississippi, resident J.T. Ross in 1935 during highway construction. *Photo by Mitch Caver*

The reverse side of the 1793 Washington peace medal found by J.T. Ross.
Photo by Mitch Caver

Brad Lieb uncovered the historical information linking the peace medals to the Chickasaws. As they and other specialists continue to uncover more clues, they may in time discover a way to determine which of the medals might have belonged to each Chickasaw leader.

It appears Wolf's Friend also died within a few years of Piominko's passing, though the circumstances remain unclear. Chickasaw interpreter Malcolm McGee recalled that Wolf's Friend took his own life in 1799 where the Duck River and the mouth of the Piney River join in middle Tennessee, where he and William Colbert had moved. McGee's account places his death not long after he lost influence in the Chickasaw Nation, after Colbert and Piominko outmaneuvered him in the fight over the fort at Chickasaw Bluffs, and on the heels of his return from a trip to Philadelphia to meet with President John Adams. McGee maintained that the onetime leader of the Spanish faction had also "long suffered with the gravel" (an apparent reference to kidney stones).[75] Thus, it is not clear from McGee's recollections whether he took his life feeling disgraced, or in excruciating pain from the stones, or from some other motivation. In this case, McGee's recollection of dates, given in 1841, years after the events occurred, may also have been slightly diminished. Other records indicate Wolf's Friend penned a letter to General James Winchester in August of 1800 about the creation of the planned Natchez Trace.[76] Several newspapers also reported his death occurred in late spring 1803, saying his suicide resulted from "a fit of remorse for having killed a young Indian in a drunken frolic."[77] It is quite possible that 1803 is the correct year, and that while Wolf's Friend suffered from kidney stones and depression, McGee chose not to include details about why he shot himself, out of respect.

George Washington, who only a few years earlier had entertained Piominko in Philadelphia and bestowed upon him the peace medal he may have been buried in, died December 14, 1799, from an undetermined, rapidly moving infection that started as a sore throat with cold symptoms.

William and George Colbert took over the reins of leadership following Piominko's death and served the Chickasaw Nation in that capacity for the next several decades. James Robertson lived about fifteen years longer than his friend Piominko and died at the Chickasaw Agency in Houlka, Mississippi, in 1814. While Piominko's physical body may have died, his indomitable spirit never did. It lives on the hearts and minds of the Chickasaw People, and in the steadfast resolve of the tribe today.

---

75. Atkinson, *Splendid Land, Splendid People*, 181-182, 197.

76. "Correspondence Between the Head Men of the Chickasaw Indians, and Gen. Winchester," *Tennessee Gazette* (Nashville), October 22, 1800, Vol. 1, Issue 34, Page 2.

77. *Independent Gazetteer* (Lexington, Kentucky), April 26, 1803, Vol. 1, No. 5, Fifth Column, Page 2; *Farmer's Weekly Museum* (Walpole, NH), May 24, 1803, Vol. XI, Issue 529, Page 3.

CHAPTER FIVE

MEMORIALIZING A CHICKASAW VISIONARY

"In compliment to Piomingo, one of the Indian chiefs, a man greatly beloved and respected, not only by the Indian tribes but also by the whites."

- Rev. Winterbotham, Baptist minister, political activist, and author, writing in 1819 about a planned township to be named for Piominko

PIOMINKO watched in awe as the new ship the *William Penn* launched in May 1791 from Philadelphia, sailing south along the Delaware River to the Atlantic Ocean, on its maiden voyage bound for London. Besides bearing the name of the famous Quaker who founded the Pennsylvania Colony, the ship was destined to become the first under the new United States flag to dock on England's Thames River since the end of the Revolutionary War. Piominko's interest in the ship included a more personal matter. On the bow of the boat was a large, detailed wooden figurehead in his "exact" likeness, strongly believed by a number of experts to be carved by the renowned American sculptor William Rush. The London newspaper *The Public Advertiser or Political and Literary Diary* later reported the event:

> The William Penn, now lying at Iron-gate Stairs, is allowed to be the finest American vessel that ever appeared in the River. She is built entirely of cedar, and carries 300 tons. The figure of the Indian and his dog on her head is said to be an exact representation of Piamingo, Chief

of the Chickasaws, now living. As she was the first vessel that ever he saw, he attended the building of her from the moment her keel was laid, till she was launched; and the moment he saw her descend to the waves set up the most dismal howl, which was immediately succeeded by the most immoderate transports of joy, when he saw that she did not sink.[1]

Owned by Philadelphia Quaker merchants Jesse and Robert Waln and John Field and Son, the *William Penn* carried both passengers and freight. Seasoned sailing master Woolman Sutton skippered the ship on her first voyage and returned to Philadelphia by that September. With Sutton now ailing, James Josiah, another highly skilled Philadelphia mariner and a friend of popular portrait artist Charles Willson Peale, would be the *Penn's* captain. Built out of cedar and live oak the *Penn* held three hundred and fifty-six tons burden, which represented a sizeable carrying capacity for its day.[2] After the ship docked in 1791 at the Irongate Stairs landing on the north side of the Thames River just downstream from the Tower of London and near the Tower Bridge, not far from where St. Katherine Docks are located today, onlookers gathered to see it, prompting a London newspaper reporter to write,

> The William Penn, at present lying in the river, is the largest vessel built in America since the Revolution. She has the figure of a Quaker on her stern, and a Savage on her stem. Her timbers are cedar, which yields a most agreeable, odor.[3]

Worried by the attention, the *Penn's* crew stood watch around the clock.

Captain Josiah's wife, Elizabeth, traveled with him on his first voyage on the *Penn*. Years later she described the resentment of many Londoners at seeing a boat with an American flag in their port. After several English women challenged her concerning what they took to be the arrogance of displaying the flag on a boat so soon after the war, she said she responded, "We win gold and wear it!"[4]

It is both symbolically and literally fitting, and ironic, that the "Savage" figurehead on the bow that led the first United States ship to enter the Port of London after the war featured the Chickasaw Nation's most distinguished

---

1. *Public Advertiser or Political and Literary Diary* (London), January 24, 1794; Reprinted in *Philadelphia Gazette*, April 28, 1794, Vol. XI, Issue 1730, Page 3, Fourth Column.

2. William Bell Clark, "James Josiah, Master Mariner," *Pennsylvania Magazine of History and Biography* 79, no. 4 (October 1955): 471.

3. *St. James Chronicle, or British Evening Post*, From Saturday, January 28 to Tuesday, January 31, 1792, Issue 4812, Page 4, Fourth Column.

4. John F. Watson, *Annals of Philadelphia and Pennsylvania Olden Time, Vol. II* (Carlisle, MA: Applewood Books, 1844), 333.

James Josiah captained the *William Penn* throughout most of the 1790s. The *Penn's* figurehead is thought to have been carved in the likeness of Piominko by renowned American sculptor William Rush. *By Charles Willson Peale, photo courtesy of Peter and Bonnie McCausland*

warrior. In that way, appropriately, Piominko's likeness signified the circular relationship of the Chickasaw Nation with the mother country and its rebellious colony. Chickasaws had generally partnered with England before the war, and Piominko offered unwavering loyalty to America after it.

In the nearly ten years of known history of the *William Penn* with its unique figurehead, the ship appears to have fostered interest everywhere it went. John Fanning Watson, author of the *Annals of Philadelphia* and an admirer of William Rush, one of America's first, and most gifted and celebrated sculptors, noted the tremendous excitement in London and elsewhere it docked. He wrote that rowboats filled with carvers drew close to the figure of the "Indian Trader...dressed in Indian habiliments" to sketch images from it or take plaster casts of its head. Watson saw the figurehead as a national treasure deserving of a wide audience, writing, "a fine Indian figure, in Rush's best style, might be preserved in some public edifice for many centuries to come."[5] While on a voyage in 1798, the French privateer ship *Voltaire* captured the unarmed *William Penn* during the Quasi-War between France and the United States, removed the crew except for Josiah, and ordered him to sail to Bordeaux, France. En route the British frigate *Cleopatra* rescued the *Penn* from the French pirates and an English convoy led the ship safely to Portsmouth, England.[6] In an emblematic sense, the spirit of Piominko imbued in the figurehead would have cringed at the prospect of being held captive in a French port, a home of historical adversaries of the Chickasaws. Equally symbolic is that an English ship helped liberate it.

Rush learned the craft of carving where he grew up in Philadelphia, a hub for shipbuilding and the nation's temporary first capital. For nearly five decades he carved numerous ship figureheads, stern ornaments, and other sculptures featuring a variety of individuals and symbolic themes. By the time the US Constitution was ratified in 1788, he was considered the country's premier carver. When Congress created the US Navy in 1794, he was commissioned to design six symbolic figureheads representing its revolutionary political ideals for new frigates. Rush, his friend Peale, and others also created the acclaimed Pennsylvania Academy of Fine Arts. After the Embargo Act of 1807 effectively destroyed the shipbuilding industry in Philadelphia, Rush turned from figureheads to creating architectural works and producing allegorical figures and busts in wood, terra-cotta, and plaster.[7]

---

5. John F. Watson, *Annals of Philadelphia and Pennsylvania Olden Time, Vol. I* (Philadelphia: Author, 1850), 576.

6. Clark, "James Josiah, Master Mariner," 478.

7. Susan James-Gadzinski, "William Rush," *American National Biography* 1, (2010), EBSCO Biography Reference Center; Ralph Sessions, "William Rush and The American Figurehead," *The Magazine Antiques* 168, no. 5 (2005): 148-153, EBSCO MasterFILE Premier.

The figurehead carved in Piominko's likeness on the bow of the *William Penn. Sketch by James Blackburn*

While conducting research for this book, author Mitch Caver stumbled across obscure newspaper articles from the 1790s, all mentioning that Piominko modeled for the carving, watched construction of the *Penn*, and saw it off on its maiden voyage with his likeness on the bow. That startling and exciting discovery led to tracking down information on the history of the *Penn* and its important figurehead. Like most other Rush figureheads, odds were long against its survival over two centuries later, but providence directed otherwise. Sometime after 1802, the *Penn* was sold in Europe, and later owners decommissioned it. There a ship salvage yard likely stripped it and sold useable parts from the boat. In time, a family in Belgium acquired the figurehead and put it to use as a garden statue. By then it had lost some of its original pieces.

The unique sculpture turned up for sale in 1985 in California. While looking at an advertisement for the San Francisco auction house Butterfield and Butterfield, antique dealer Peter Hill noticed the badly damaged and poorly restored figurehead. Moreover, he suspected it had been miscataloged. Having attended the Pennsylvania Academy of Fine Arts, Hill believed Rush may have carved it, while the auction house, lacking any good provenance, had listed its carver as French. After consulting with friends concerning his suspicions, Hill flew to California and purchased it for $18,000 at auction. He then consulted about it with a former business associate, conservator Mark Adams. Adams assembled a team including a naval architectural specialist, a conservator for the Smithsonian Institution, an art historian, an Eastern Woodland Native American expert, an interpreter, researchers, and others. Hill, Adams, and their cohorts spent years examining every inch of the seven-and-half-foot-tall sculpture, including paint traces on it. They determined its eighteenth-century authenticity and concluded there was a high probability that Rush carved it.[8]

As a result, in 1996 Adams and Melvin Wachowiak Jr., the Smithsonian conservator, contributed to a book, published by Hill, that presented a comparative study of Rush's other surviving carvings with the *Penn's* figurehead. By examining Rush's unique style of carving ears, eyes, head and body features, feathers, animal heads, bow knots, fabric, scrolls, and other distinct features, he presented a compelling case for its similarities to Rush's other works.[9] Sylvia Leistyna Lahvis, the art historian on the project, said every feature on

---

8. Mary Jo Lipman, "Work of Art – and a Snub to the Crown? Antiques Dealer finds Monumental American Sculpture," July 2, 1999, CNN.com, www.cnn.com/STYLE/9907/02/rush.sculpture/index.html; Sylvia Leistyna Lahvis, "William Rush: Indian Trader," *The Magazine Antiques* 156, no. 6 (December 1999): 846-852; Mike Recht, "With Antique Figurehead at the Prow, a Million Dreams Set Sail," *Los Angeles Times*, February 27, 2000, http://articles.latimes.com/2000/feb/27/news/mn-3151.

9. Peter Hill, *Signatures of Style: Introducing Tamanend, An Allegorical Figure of the New Republic* (P. Hill, 2001).

William Rush, one of America's first and most gifted and celebrated sculptors, is believed to have created this figure-head of Piominko for the *William Penn* around 1791. *Photo courtesy of Tony Choate*

Photo courtesy of Tony Choate

Photo courtesy of Tony Choate

Chickasaw Nation Secretary of Culture and Humanities Lisa John with the figure-head during a viewing in New Hampshire in 2014. *Photo courtesy of Tony Choate*

the sculpture, carved almost entirely from a single white pine log, is allegorical, in typical Rush style, and an important American iconic symbol of an emerging nation.

> The fact he's returning from the hunt ... symbolizes freedom. His prize of a rabbit, displayed in his right hand, is a metaphor for the new nation's bounty. The dog leaping at his feet shows loyalty, and the oak pushing from the rock signifies strength.[10]

If Hill's modest purchase in 1985, now owned by Adams Inc., is in fact one of the last surviving Rush pieces, it is perhaps worth millions. George Gurney, deputy chief curator for the Smithsonian's National Museum of American Art, commented in 2000 after viewing it that he had high confidence of its authenticity. It may be impossible to prove with complete assurance that Rush carved it, he said, but "It's hard to ignore it. It's a very imposing figure." To fully appreciate the beauty of the piece and help conceptualize the restoration proposals, Adam's team created a replica of it in clay with the missing pieces restored.[11]

However, Adams and his team still had little information regarding the Native American subject of the carving. Unaware of the evidence for its possible connection to Piominko, some members of the team speculated that it represented noted Delaware (Lenni-Lanape) chief Tamanend (or Tammany or Tammamend), who befriended William Penn in the early days of the Pennsylvania Colony. During the early years of the United States, in places like Philadelphia, Tamanend was regarded as a folk hero and distinct symbol of the new nation. Admirers created sculptures, festivals and operas, and made references to him in fiction. Certainly Rush would have been familiar with his story, as his popularity peaked about the time Rush was carving in Philadelphia. At first glance it is an exceptionally logical assumption, particularly since it graced the bow of the *William Penn*. Convinced of that possibility, Hill published two small booklets, *Signatures of Style* and *Tamanend, the Indian Trader: Icon of the New Nation*, attributing the likeness of his recently purchased figurehead to the Delaware peacemaker. Hill's and others' later use of the designation "Indian Trader" appears to come from the title for the figurehead that Watson coined for his readers 1830.

When Caver saw a newspaper article in 2000 that recounted Hill's purchase of the figurehead, Adams' research team's conclusion that Rush likely carved it, and that it once adorned the *William Penn*, it aroused his curiosity. Moreover, photos that accompanied the article, showing the figurehead in ap-

---

10. Quoted in Lipman, "Work of Art – and a Snub to the Crown?" CNN.com.
11. Mike Recht, "With Antique Figurehead at the Prow, a Million Dreams Set Sail" *Los Angeles Times*, February 27, 2000.

propriate period cultural dress alongside a dog, closely matched descriptions in the 1790s newspaper accounts he had found about Piominko posing for the sculpture. Those and other details raised the possibility the figurehead in the more recent article was the same as the one in the eighteenth-century newspaper stories. Native American specialists studying the figurehead had determined Rush used a live model because it perfectly depicted period cultural Woodlands dress, from the leggings and tinkler cones to arm bands and hair adornments. In many ways, it mirrors Presbyterian Missionary Joseph Bullen's description of the dress of Chickasaw men when he visited Wolf's Friend in Chisha' Talla'a' in 1800.

> One bunch of hair is tied on the top of the head, to which is fastened, in seven locks, enclosed in silver and beads, the hair of a deer's tail coloured red: this hangs over the face and eyes; the face is painted with streaks and spots of red and black; the beard is pulled out; the neck adorned with a dozen strings of beads of different sorts besides a silk handkerchief; the arms and wrists adorned with silver bands; the body and arms covered with a calico shirt; the dress of the lower limbs is various. ...The men have a bunch of white feathers fastened to the back part of the neck, and if a person of note, a black feather; and lest the dress or colouring should be discomposed, carries his glass in his pocket, or hanging to his side.[12]

After contacting several museums and curators, Caver tracked down Adams to inquire about the prized figurehead. At the invitation of Mark and Wendy Adams, a small group of Chickasaw Nation officials, including Chickasaw Secretary of Culture and Humanities Lisa John, traveled with Caver to see it in person in March 2014.

Adams and other specialists who have spent years researching the figurehead believe with a high degree of certainty that it represents not only Piominko's likeness carved by Rush, but one of America's first important symbols of liberty, and rivals icons like the Liberty Bell, Independence Hall, and others. In that sense, they see it as an exceptionally valuable historical artifact that also showcases Piominko's and the Chickasaw Nation's significant contributions to the creation of the United States in its earliest days as a republic. Today it remains in private hands. Now that good fortune resurrected it from obscurity, Adams hopes that one day it will be displayed in a prominent and appropriate museum for a large audience to see and fully appreciate it.

---

12. Cornelius Davis, ed., *New York Missionary Magazine, and Repository of Religious Intelligence for the Year 1800* (New York: T & J. Swords, 1800), 367.

Photo courtesy of Tony Choate

Conservator Mark Adams, Chickasaw Nation Secretary of Culture and Humanities Lisa John, and author Mitch Caver with the figurehead during a viewing in 2014. *Photo courtesy of Tony Choate*

Fortunately, Piominko lived to see a great boat with his incredible likeness on the bow, however, there would be many other tributes to him created after his death that might have pleased him, too. Some sought to honor him not in a carved wooden likeness, but rather with a proposed city in Kentucky bearing his name. Pennsylvania land speculator and financier John Nicholson, a contemporary of Piominko, partnered with Robert Morris and James Greenleaf in the mid-1790s to form the large North American Land Company, with land holdings in several states that totaled six million acres. Nicholson created a separate business venture with associates from Philadelphia, Baltimore, and England to develop a 100,000-acre tract near Louisville, Kentucky, which he referred to as "Piomingo." He and his colleagues recognized Piominko's contributions toward helping the new country to get off the ground. Nicholson hired agents to sell individual plots of the planned development to prospective buyers in England and the British Isles. Within the "Piomingo Tract," Nicholson envisioned three communities: Lystra, Frankenville, and Ohiopiomingo. Blueprints for the communities looked exceptionally similar to the layout of the federal city in Washington, D.C.[13] Nicholson and his partners named Ohiopiomingo as a "compliment to Piomingo ... a man greatly beloved and respected, not only by the Indian tribes but also by the whites."[14] He proposed to build the new town on a slight bluff, near present-day West Point, Kentucky, overlooking the Ohio River, less than thirty miles south of Louisville. Appropriately, its originators visualized in the center of the city a high-quality Coade stone statue of Piominko "delivering an oration in favour of Liberty." Nicholson's enterprising vision called for more than a thousand houses on forty-three streets, with each house situated on a one-hundred-by-three-hundred-foot lot, and fields of five or twenty acres. Each farmer-settler was to receive five hundred acres on a ninety-nine-year lease. The acreage came rent-free for the first three years, provided the settlers built their houses and barns within that time, besides planting at least twenty acres of crops. Nicholson and his cohorts conceptualized the project as containing several capital squares with ornate buildings, a circus, and an exceptionally progressive college for its day that would accept Native American students.[15] Unfortunately, the Piominko Tract and Ohiopiomingo development never got off the ground. Its promoters failed to generate enough sales in Europe and America. Five years after his

---

13. Robert D. Arbuckle, "Ohiopiomingo: The 'Mythical' Kentucky Settlement That Was Not a Myth," *The Register of the Kentucky Historical Society* 70, no. 4 (1972): 318-321; Rev. William Winterbotham, *An Historical, Topographical and Statistical View of the United States of America, From the Earliest Period to the Present Time*, Vol. III (London: J. Ridgway, Piccadilly, Sherwood and Co., 1819), 147-148; Wil Verhoeven, *Americomania and the French Revolution Debate, 1789-1802* (Cambridge: Cambridge University Press, 2013), 212-235.

14. Winterbotham, *An Historical, Topographical and Statistical View of the United States*, 147.

15. Ibid.

promotion of the now-bankrupt development, and other failed projects, Nicholson died in debtors' prison at 43, leaving a wife, eight children, legions of creditors, and debts totaling the astronomical sum of $12 million.[16]

However, other geographical landmarks and features would bear Piominko's name. The Natchez Trace Parkway today runs along a 444-mile two-lane scenic highway maintained by the National Park Service. Initially, however, travelers called its northern portion, which runs from near present-day Tupelo, Mississippi, to Nashville, Tennessee, "Piomingo's Trace" (or "Mountain Leader's Trace," or "Trail"). Piominko and other Chickasaws often took that trail to Nashville and the Cumberland settlements to meet US government officials, and for hunting or trade. Shortly after Piominko's death and new treaties with the Chickasaws and Choctaws, US policymakers extended the trail south to Natchez, Mississippi, and changed its name to Natchez Trace or Trail (also called the Old Natchez Trace). Today the new parkway runs a scenic route from Natchez to Nashville, and while it doesn't always follow the old Trace route, it is similar to the one traders, explorers, emigrants, and Native Americans, including Piominko, used for several centuries.[17] Just off the Natchez Trace Parkway, "Lake Piomingo" is a 115-acre private lake for a subdivision about ten miles northeast of Tupelo, near Saltillo, in Lee County, Mississippi.

Over a century ago other enthusiasts suggested an "Indian mound" or museum in present-day Sulphur, Oklahoma, would be the most appropriate way to honor the Chickasaw patriot. Because of the popularity of more than thirty mineral springs in the Sulphur area, developers in the early 1900s envisioned creating a resort town in Indian Territory to rival Hot Springs, Arkansas. In 1902, after its purchase of a square mile of land from the Chickasaw and Choctaw Nations, the US government created Sulphur Springs Reservation. Congress bought more acreage shortly thereafter, and in 1906 designated the area as Platt National Park, with Colonel Joseph F. Swords serving as its first superintendent.[18] Swords proposed to the Chickasaw Nation in 1902 that with the creation of the new Sulphur Springs Reservation they should build an "Indian mound" within it atop Bromide Hill as a fitting tribute to the legacy and memory of Piominko. Apparently lacking funding, US policymakers and Chickasaw officials never constructed the memorial.[19] In 1976 National Park officials combined Platt National Park and Arbuckle Recreation Area to form

---

16. Arbuckle, "Ohiopiomingo: The 'Mythical' Kentucky Settlement That Was Not a Myth," 321.

17. "History of the Natchez Trace," Natchez Trace Parkway Association, http://natcheztrace.org/history-of-the-natchez-trace/.

18. Constance A. Rudd, "Chickasaw National Recreation Area," *The Encyclopedia of Oklahoma History and Culture,* www.okhistory.org.

19. "Mound to Indian's Memory," *The St. Louis Republic,* Part I, June 22, 1902, Page 2.

This map of Kentucky and the southeastern United States from the 1790s shows geographic features and place names bearing Piominko's title during that time period. *Courtesy of David Rumsey Map Collection, davidrumsey.com*

Above:
A 115-acre private lake named for Piominko is located about ten miles northeast of Tupelo, near Saltillo, in Lee County, Mississippi. Various roads around the lake also have historic Chickasaw names. *Photo by Mitch Caver*

Left:
In 1976 National Park officials combined Platt National Park and Arbuckle Recreation Area to form the Chickasaw National Recreation Area in Sulphur, Oklahoma. *Photo by Branden Hart*

the Chickasaw National Recreation Area.

In a similar vein, a representative of Andrew Carnegie in 1909 suggested the philanthropist's willingness to provide significant funds to help build a Native American museum in the newly created national park. Evidently, the proposal grew out of the need for a place to properly display a captain's commission that Secretary of War Henry Knox and President George Washington gave on June 25, 1794, to Chickasaw "Chief Muckleshamingo" to raise a company to fight in General Anthony Wayne's campaign. Muckleshamingo (Mucklesa Minko, or Imoklaasha' Minko') represented the title of the civil minko of the revered Chickasaw Imoklaasha' kinship, and traveled with Piominko and others for their meeting in Philadelphia with the president and Knox.[20] Somehow Indian Territory Judge George W. Hawkins, a Choctaw leader, acquired the well-preserved sheepskin commission. On his deathbed, Hawkins bequeathed it to former Chickasaw Governor William M. Guy, with specific instructions that he "carefully preserve and guard it until the Chickasaw or Five Tribes combined, aided by some millionaire or millionaires build an Indian museum in the Five Tribes country."[21] Hope arose when *The Dallas Morning News* reported in 1909 that the leaders of the Five Tribes discovered:

> from a representative of Andrew Carnegie that he will give a large sum for the museum building providing that Congress will set apart suitable grounds for the structure in Platt National Park, and provided the United States will take charge of the building after its completion and maintain it throughout all of time. In case the chiefs of the Five Tribes fail to interest Mr. Carnegie and Congress and interest will be made to induce the State to aid them in the construction of the museum, the museum to be a State instead of National intuition, and be maintained by the State, the United States to cede to Oklahoma, a suitable site in Platt Park for the structure.[22]

Mrs. W. L. Ingram, Governor Guy's niece, lacked the means to properly display or preserve the commission in the absence of a state Native American museum, so in 1921 she "deposited it with" the Oklahoma Historical Society for safekeeping.[23] It remains today at the society's new history center across the street from the Oklahoma State Capitol and represents one of last remaining relics from Piominko's historic 1794 meeting with Washington in Philadelphia.

---

20. John Dyson, email message to Tom Cowger, June 23, 2016.
21. "Indian Chief's Commission Signed by President George Washington," *Dallas Morning News*, September 21, 1909, Vol. XXIV, No. 356, Page 10.
22. Ibid.
23. "Historical News Items," *Chronicles of Oklahoma* 1, no. 1 (January 1921): 109.

Piominko would have received an identical commission on that same trip.

Several artists have used their talents to commemorate the "Mountain Leader" in bronze. Rotary Club in Tupelo, Mississippi, commissioned sculptor and former University of Mississippi adjunct assistant professor of art William "Bill" Beckwith to create a sculpture of Piominko that now stands in front of the City Hall in Tupelo. At its unveiling in 2005, Kirk Perry, then administrator of heritage preservation for the Chickasaw Nation, remarked, "the Chickasaws have been removed here for roughly one hundred seventy years, and it is significant now to remember our father of this country."[24] Beckwith, most known for his portrait busts of notable figures, took a little over a year to produce the statue. His work is held in private collections throughout the nation as well as several permanent ones. He resides in Taylor, Mississippi, where he operates a sculpture studio.[25] Like any other artist would, Beckwith struggled to create a likeness of Piominko without an actual image to work with. He turned to several individuals at the Chickasaw Nation and scholars and historians for help. He also poured over all written material he could find on Piominko, histories of the period, and Chickasaw and Southeastern tribal histories to be as culturally sensitive and historically accurate as possible. While he worked on the piece, he surrounded himself with cultural artifacts to set the mood while he crafted it.[26] In the end, he said, "the rest had to come from Piomingo himself. He revealed himself slowly." As the image came to him, he chose to depict him,

> In his later years, probably in his fifties. I put him in a coat that George Washington gave to him – a military coat that the Indians called the "great coat." I put his hair down and put two small braids in the front, which some of the drawings show. He is also wearing the "great shirt" – a long shirt about knee-length gathered with a sash tied at the waist. On the sash, they would have some emblems from their clan, but I didn't try to do that because I didn't know what they would be. He's also wearing moccasins and leather leggings.[27]

---

24. "Tupelo Dedicates Piominko Statue, 2005," Chickasaw Nation, www.chickasaw.tv.

25. "Bill Beckwith, Faculty Emeritus," University of Mississippi, College of Liberal Arts, Department of Art and History, http://art.olemiss.edu/2012/07/10/bill-beckwith/.

26. Ashley Elkins, "Piomingo Revealed Himself to Artist," *Northeast Mississippi Daily Journal*, August 16, 2005, http://djournal.com/news/piomingo-revealed-himself-to-artist/; "Keeping Piominko's Memory Alive: Bill Beckwith," Chickasaw Nation video, 1:34, and "Tupelo's Piomingo Statue Takes Shape: Greg Pirkle" Chickasaw Nation video, 2:04, both at www.chickasaw.tv.

27. Elkins, "Piomingo Revealed Himself to Artist," *Northeast Mississippi Daily Journal*, August 16, 2005.

A bronze sculpture of Piominko was commissioned by the Rotary Club in Tupelo, Mississippi, in 2005. William Beckwith, adjunct assistant professor of art at the University of Mississippi, sculpted the bronze figure which now stands in front of the Tupelo city hall. Beckwith consulted with the Chickasaw Nation during his creation of the sculpture. *Photo by Jacquelyn Sparks*

Seminole Nation Principal Chief Enoch Kelly Haney sculpted this bronze statue of Pi-ominko that stands in front of the historic Chickasaw National Capitol in Tishomingo, Oklahoma. The statue was formally dedicated on April 28, 2014, by Chickasaw Nation Governor Bill Anoatubby and Lt. Governor Jefferson Keel. *Photo by Wakeah Vigil*

Beckwith commented that working on the statue fundamentally changed him in a positive way that he cannot fully explain. When he brought the finished sculpture home from a foundry in Florida and got closer to the Chickasaw Homeland, he said, "he envisioned Chickasaw warriors along the side of the road welcoming the chief back to Tupelo."[28]

Two other artists used bronze as the medium to depict him. Internationally recognized artist and former Seminole Nation Principal Chief and Oklahoma state politician Enoch Kelly Haney spent over three years creating a sculpture of Piominko that now stands watch over the historic Chickasaw Nation Capitol Building in Tishomingo, Oklahoma. Governor Bill Anoatubby presided over its dedication on April 28, 2014.

Recognizing Piominko's indispensable place in Memphis and Tennessee history, the Memphis-based First Tennessee Bank in 1983 commissioned artist Roy Tamboli to create a bronze of him. Created in a figurative and somewhat abstract style, it remains on display in the bank's headquarters in Memphis. When completed in 1985 it fulfilled historian Samuel Cole William's challenge from 1930 that "historic Justice will not be done until in Memphis there stands a statue to the great chief of the Chickasaws, Piomingo."[29] Chickasaw Governor Overton James attended the unveiling of the sculpture. Memphis also has a street named after Piominko, and several Tennessee organizations have honored him with namesake chapters, including the Chief Piomingo Chapter of the United States Daughters of the American Revolution in Collierville, and the Piomingo Chapter of the United States Daughters of 1812 in Millington.

Other memorialists turned to the written word. Longtime Nashville resident and schoolteacher Lizzie P. Elliott described Piominko in her 1911 book, *Early History of Nashville*. Intended as a textbook for young people, the book is a mixture of grounded history and imagination. Written in somewhat of a romantic and nostalgic style, the section on Piominko is no exception. While attempting to portray Piominko in a positive light, it inadvertently comes across sometimes as ethnocentric, not unlike other books of the period. At the same time, it is clear that she and the generation of Nashville residents before her appreciated Piominko's efforts on their behalf in the American settlement of the Cumberland area and wanted to ensure later ones did as well. Near the end of her narrative on him, she summarized his importance for the younger readers.

"Well," Colonel Robertson said, "I think we can trust Piomingo. He is our friend. The Chickasaws of his village,

---

28. Keeping Piominko's Memory Alive," and "Tupelo Piomingo Statue Takes Shape," www.chickasaw.tv.

29. Samuel Cole Williams, *Beginnings of West Tennessee in the Land of the Chickasaws, 1541-1841* (Johnson City, TN: Watauga Press, 1930), 59.

First Tennessee Bank commissioned Roy Tamboli to create this bronze of Piominko in 1983. Finished in 1985, it now stands in the First Tennessee Bank in Memphis, Tennessee. Chickasaw Governor Overton James attended the statue's unveiling in Memphis. *Photo courtesy of Roy Tamboli*

at least, will be our friends. He will keep his word. He is a grand old Indian." ... The Stationers at the Bluff learned much from him that helped them to know what to do.... This helped not only to save the lives of the people, but helped them to keep this land here at the Bluff for their own and to begin the city of Nashville, and even to keep this land a part of the United States that was to be. So the men at the Bluff valued the friendship of Piomingo, the Mountain Leader.[30]

The book also contained a pencil sketch of unknown origin depicting Piominko's face. Shortly after Piominko's death, author John Robinson in 1810 appropriated his name as a pseudonym to write a series of essays entitled *The Savage*.[31] The essays bear little connection to the historical figure whose name Robinson so freely borrowed.

While Elliott tried to create a narrative portrait of Piominko's place in history, others turned to canvas or sketch paper. In the 1950s, real estate broker and former longtime Tupelo and Lee County, Mississippi, Community Development Foundation president Harry A. Martin commissioned artist Wade Herbert Armstrong to paint a portrait of Piominko that Martin proudly hung in his Tupelo home.[32] Perhaps far and away the most important drawing is by an undisclosed artist. In a recent ebay search, author Tom Cowger stumbled on a rare piece of stationery that sparked his and Caver's curiosity. During the 1920s the Hotel Chisca in Memphis issued stationery bearing a portrait of Piominko taken "from an authentic sketch from life" as a nod to the history of the location of the hotel. While there is no attribution to the source of the drawing or how the hotel acquired it, it looks like it could have come from a long-lost sketch of him that he sat for. Several factors suggest both the historical importance of the image and the possibility it is an actual sketch of him. Among these are that it exhibits noteworthy similarity to the only other known sketch of an unknown Chickasaw male, and Piominko contemporary, made in 1775 by surveyor, naturalist, and author Bernard Romans. For example, the single feather of the Hotel Chisca sketch matches the placement and shading of the feather in Roman's sketch. The Presbyterian missionary Bullen wrote that the color and placement of the feather is critical, as they can signify a Chickasaw person of great note.[33] Both sketches are of individuals of high status, but the

---

30. Lizzie P. Elliott, *Early History of Nashville* (Nashville, TN: Ambrose Printing Company, 1911), 182-183.

31. Piomingo, *The Savage* (Philadelphia: T. Cadell and W. Davies, Strand, 1810).

32. "Piomingo, the Mountain Leader," *Journal of Chickasaw History* 8, no. 1, Series 29 (2002): 4.

33. "Excerpts from the Journal of the Reverend Joseph Bullen, 1799 and 1800," *Journal of Mississippi History* 17 (October 1955): 273-274.

This stationery issued by the Hotel Chisca in Memphis, Tennessee, in the 1920s features a portrait of Piominko, which it claims is "from an authentic sketch from life." The portrait was likely intended to be a nod to the history of the location of the hotel.

facial features and a few other minor details are different. The drawing also bears a striking resemblance to the figurehead. The intricate design on the headband in the sketch is a unique design and identical to the one on the sash belt of the figurehead. Few, if any, twentieth-century artists would have had familiarity with that specific pattern. The facial features are also exceptionally similar. In the sketch Piominko is depicted as wearing a single strand of white, or light-colored, beads like those he often gave away as gifts. Except for contemporaries, few knew such details. When the hotel sketch is compared to the one Romans drew, and the figurehead, the similarities are unavoidable and seem nearly beyond coincidence. This leads to our belief that it could be an actual representation of Piominko. The only other plausible explanation is that an artist hired by the hotel in the 1920s created a new marketing logo of Piominko by altering the Romans sketch, but that seems highly unlikely. The artist would not have known other previously mentioned details or similarities to the figurehead.

Other namesakes, and a Chickasaw holiday also memorialize Piominko. Less than forty-five miles southwest of Louisville on the Ohio River in Brandenburg, Kentucky, YMCA officials created Camp Piomingo more than seventy years ago as a place for youth to explore nature and "make lifelong memories — all in a safe, caring, friendly environment."[34] In a strange and ironic twist, the future president and architect of Indian Removal, Andrew Jackson, who had many land dealings concerning the creation of Memphis, by 1800 had named one of his favorite horses "Piomingo."[35] Jackson saw it as a tribute to the important legacy of the Chickasaw war minko and his loyalty to America. Unfortunately, his later removal policies did not return the favor to the Chickasaws for their valued service in the creation of the country. In lieu of observing Columbus Day, the Chickasaw Nation since 2008 has celebrated Piominko Day on the second Monday of each October.

As Piominko enjoyed his last healthy days in Chokka' Falaa', he may not have fully understood his important place in history, but he certainly would have known the results of his leadership. For several decades Piominko stood at the diplomatic intersection of competing European, and later American, interests that recognized the Chickasaws' influence and power and courted their allegiance. Much like a skilled navigator, Piominko had steered the Chickasaws through turbulent times and stormy waters that threatened to undermine the authority of the Nation and divide it. He also survived several attempts on his life by competing outsiders whose visions differed from his.

---

34. "The YMCA: Camp Piomingo," http://ymcacamppiomingo.org.
35. Andrew Jackson to Robert Hays, 18 February 1800, in *The Papers of Andrew Jackson, 1770-1803*, Vol. 1, ed. Sam B. Smith and Harriet Chappell Owsley (Knoxville: University of Tennessee Press, 1980), 227.

Under his leadership, the Chickasaws managed to maintain their sovereignty and independence, and he never sold or parted with a single acre of Chickasaw land. He more than lived up to his title and was a Chickasaw visionary in war and peace. America owes him a large debt of gratitude that may be impossible to repay. The least that ought to be done, however, is to mark his importance in American history. He helped the United States secure control of the Mississippi and Cumberland Valleys, which ensured the success of the new country. Former Memphis mayor and judge James H. Malone, in his book on the Chickasaw Nation in 1922, nicely summarized Piominko's significance this way:

> If the intellectual capacities of men are to be controlled by their natural and climatic environment, then, as the Indians of America were, so to speak, natural products of the respective localities, attention is called to the fact that Piomingo, the un-lettered full-blooded Chickasaw chief proved to be a worthy match for the Spanish and French diplomats; and that whether on the field of battle, or in the arena of diplomacy, he withstood all the wiles of those opposed to the Americans, including the seductive influence of money. Did he not possess a wonderful judgment of men, not to say prescience of the future, when he chose on all occasions, and under the most adverse circumstances, to bend his people to the cause of the Americans rather than to that of France or Spain? [36]

Piominko's greatest legacy, however, is not in prose, bronze, canvas, proposed cities, namesakes, presidential medals, commissions, or meetings with America's first president, but in his incomparable spirit reflected today in the enduring resolve of his people and their relentless defense of sovereignty and protection of Chickasaw interests. His energy, spirit, and vision remain the pulse and heartbeat of his nation today. He is the epitome of the "unconquered and unconquerable."

---

36. James H. Malone, *The Chickasaw Nation: A Short Sketch of a Noble People* (Louisville, KY: John. P. Morton & Co., 1922), 369.

BIBLIOGRAPHY

Adams, Charles Frances, ed. *Memoirs of John Quincy Adams: Comprising Portions of His Diary, From 1795-1848, Vol. I.* Philadelphia: J.B. Lippencott & Co., 1874.

Albright, Edward. *Early History of Middle Tennessee.* Nashville, TN: Brandon Printing Company, 1909.

American State Papers. Indian Affairs, Vol. 1, 1789-1814.

————. Foreign Relations, Vol. 1, 1789-1797.

Arbuckle, Robert D. "Ohiopiomingo: The 'Mythical' Kentucky Settlement That Was Not a Myth." *The Register of the Kentucky Historical Society* 70, no. 4 (1972): 318-21.

Atkinson, James R. "Death of A Chickasaw Leader: Probable Grave of Piomingo." *Mississippi Archaeology* 35, no 2. (Winter 2000):124-72.

————. "A Narrative Based on an Interview with Malcolm McGee by Lyman C. Draper," *Journal of Mississippi History* 66 (Spring 2004): 37-74.

————. *Splendid Land, Splendid People: The Chickasaw Indians to Removal.* Tuscaloosa: University of Alabama Press, 2004.

Baird, David. W. *The Chickasaw People.* Phoenix: Indian Tribal Series, 1975.

Barnett, James F., Jr. *Mississippi's American Indians.* Jackson: University of Mississippi Press, 2012.

Bays, Bill. *James Robertson, Father of Tennessee and Founder of Nashville.* Bloomington, IN: WestBow Press, 2013.

Belden, Bauman L. *Indian Peace Medals Issued in the United States.* New Milford, CT: N. Flayderman, 1966.

Bergeron, Paul, Stephen V. Ash, and Jeanette Keith. *Tennesseans and their History.* Knoxville: University of Tennessee Press, 1999.

Braden, Guy B. "The Colberts and the Chickasaw Nation." *Tennessee Historical Quarterly* 17 no. 3 (September 1958): 222-249, and no. 4 (December 1958): 318-335.

Calloway, Colin G. *The American Revolution in Indian Country: Crisis and Diversity in Native American Communities.* Cambridge: Cambridge University Press, 1995.

Cashin, Edward J. *Guardians of the Valley: Chickasaws in Colonial South Carolina and Georgia.* Columbia: University of South Carolina Press, 2009.

Caughey, John Walton. *McGillivray of the Creeks.* Norman: University of Oklahoma Press, 1938.

Clark, Walter, ed. *The State Records of North Carolina, Vol. XVII, 1781-85.* Goldsboro, NC: 1899.

Clark, William. "James Josiah, Master Mariner," *Pennsylvania Magazine of History and*

Biography 79, Issue 4 (October 1955): 452-484.

Clayton, W.W. *History of Davidson County, Tennessee, with Illustrations and Biographical Sketches of its Prominent Men and Pioneers.* Philadelphia, PA: J.W. Lewis & Co., 1880.

Coker, William, and Thomas D. Watson. *Indian Traders of the Southeastern Spanish Borderlands: Panton, Leslie & Company and John Forbes & Company, 1783-1847.* Pensacola: University Press of Florida, 1986.

Cotterill, Robert S. *The Southern Indians: The Story of the Civilized Tribes Before Removal.* Norman: University of Oklahoma Press, 1954.

———. "The Virginia-Chickasaw Treaty of 1783." *The Journal of Southern History* 8, no. 4 (1942): 483-96.

Cravatt, Matthew, ed. "Piomingo, the Mountain Leader," *Journal of Chickasaw History* 8, no.1, Series 29 (2002): 4-5.

Cushman, H. B., and Angie Debo. *History of the Choctaw, Chickasaw, and Natchez Indians.* Norman: University of Oklahoma Press, 1999.

Davis, Cornelius, ed. *New York Missionary Magazine, and Repository of Religious Intelligence for the Year 1800.* New York: T. & J. Swords, 1800.

Draper, Lyman. "Life of Boone" (Unfinished Manuscript) Draper Manuscript Collection, 3 B 47-53, State Historical Society of Wisconsin.

DuVal, Kathleen. *Independence Lost: Lives on the Edge of the American Revolution.* New York: Random House, 2015.

Dyson, John P. "Chickasaw War Names and Four Homeland Colberts: William, George, Levi and Martin." *The Journal of Chickasaw History and Culture* 17, no. 2 (Fall 2015): 6-21.

———. *The Early Chickasaw Homeland: Origins, Boundaries and Society.* Ada, OK: Chickasaw Press, 2014.

Elliott, Lizzie P. *Early History of Nashville.* Nashville, TN: Ambrose Printing Company, 1911.

English, William Hayden. *Conquest of Country Northwest of River Ohio, 1778-1783.* Indianapolis, IN: Bowen-Merrill, 1897.

Ethridge, Robbie. *From Chicaza to Chickasaw: The European Invasion and the Transformation of the Mississippian World, 1540-1715.* Chapel Hill: University of North Carolina Press, 2010.

Ethridge, Robbie and Sherri M. Shuck-Hall, eds. *Mapping the Mississippian Shatter Zone: The Colonial Indian Slave Trade and Regional Instability in the American South.* Lincoln: University of Nebraska Press, 2009.

Fogelson, Raymond and William Sturtevant, eds. *Handbook of North American Indians, Vol. 14: Southeast.* Smithsonian Institution, September 20, 2004.

Fraser, Kathryn M. "Fort Jefferson: George Roger Clark's Fort at the Mouth of the Ohio River, 1780-1781." *Register of the Kentucky Historical Society* 81, no. 1 (Winter 1983): 1-24.

Fulsom, Charles Scrivner. *The Early Chickasaws: Profile of Courage.* New York: Vantage Press, 2005.

Gallay, Alan. *The Indian Slave Trade.* New Haven, CT: Yale University Press, 2002.

Gibson, Arrell M. *The Chickasaws.* Norman: University of Oklahoma Press, 1971.

Green, Richard. *Chickasaw Lives Volume Three: Sketches Past and Present.* Ada, OK:

Chickasaw Press, 2010.

Hamilton, Emory L. "Historical Sketches of Southwest Virginia Publication 5: The Long Hunters," Historical Society of Southwest Virginia (March 1970).

Hankla, Mel. "Riflemen of the Cumberland and the Guns That Made Them Famous." *Kentucky Rifle Association Bulletin* 40, no. 3 (Spring 2014).

Haywood, John. *The Civil and Political History of the State of Tennessee from its Earliest Settlement Up to the Year 1796, Including the Boundaries of the State.* Nashville, TN: Publishing house of the Methodist Episcopal church, South, 1891.

Heath, William. *William Wells and the Struggle for the Old Northwest.* Norman: University of Oklahoma Press, 2015.

Henry, William W. *Patrick Henry: Life, Correspondence and Speeches, Vol. 1.* New York: Burt Franklin, 1891.

Hill, Peter. *Signatures of Style: Introducing Tamanend, Allegorical Figure of the New Republic.* P. Hill, 2001.

Holms, Jack D.L. "The Ebb Tide of Spanish Military Power on the Mississippi: Fort San Fernando De Las Barrancas, 1795-1798." *East Tennessee Historical Society's Publications* 36 (1964): 23-44.

———. *Gayoso: The Life of a Spanish Governor in the Mississippi Valley, 1789-1799.* Baton Rouge: Louisiana State University Press, 1965.

———. "Spanish-American Rivalry over the Chickasaw Bluffs, 1780-1795." *East Tennessee Historical Society's Publications* 34 (1962): 26-57.

———. "Spanish Treaties with West Florida Indians, 1784-1802." *Florida Historical Quarterly* 48 (July 1969-April 1970): 140-154.

Houck, Louis, ed. *The Spanish Regime in Missouri, Vol. 1.* Chicago: Donnelley and Sons Company, 1909.

Howe, George. *History of the Presbyterian Church of South Carolina, Vol. II.* Columbia, SC: W.J. Duffie, 1883.

Howell, Robert Boyte C. *The Baptist, Vol. IV.* Nashville, TN: W.H. Dunn, 1838.

Hudson, Charles. *The Southeastern Indians.* Knoxville: University of Tennessee Press, 1976.

Hutton, Paul A. "William Wells: Frontier Scout and Indian Agent," *Indiana Magazine of History* 74, no. 3 (1978): 183-222.

Iberville, Pierre. *Iberville's Gulf Journals.* Translated and edited by Richebourg McWilliams. Tuscaloosa: University of Alabama Press, 1981.

Jackson, Andrew. *The Papers of Andrew Jackson, 1770-1803, Vol. I.* Edited by Sam B. Smith and Harriet Chappell Owsley. Knoxville: University of Tennessee Press, 1980.

James, A.R. *Standard History of Memphis, Tennessee: From a Study of the Original Sources.* Knoxville, TN: H. W. Crew, 1912.

James, James Alton, ed. *Virginia Series Volume III: George Rogers Clark Papers, 1771-1781, Vol. I.* Springfield, IL: Trustees of the Illinois State Historical Library, 1912.

James-Gadzinski, Susan. "William Rush," *American National Biography* 1, (2010). EBSCO Biography Reference Center.

Kappler, Charles J., ed. *Indian Affairs: Laws and Treaties, Vol. II.* Washington, D.C.: Government Printing Office, 1904.

Kinnaird, Lawrence. "Spain in the Mississippi Valley." *Annual Reports of the American*

Historical Association for the Year 1945. Vol. 2, Part 1 (1949); Vol. 3, Part 2 (1946); and Vol. 4, Part 3 (1946). Washington, D.C.: Government Printing Office.

———. "Spanish Treaties with Indian Tribes." *The Western Historical Quarterly* 10, no. 1 (January 1979): 39-48.

Malone, J.H. *The Chickasaw Nation: A Short Sketch of a Noble People.* Louisville, KY: John P. Morton, 1922.

Martini, Don. *The Indian Chiefs of the Southeast: A Guide, 1750-1861.* Ripley, MS: 1991.

———. *Who Was Who Among the Southern Indians: A Genealogical Notebook, 1698-1907.* Falkner, MS: Pioneer Publishing Company, 1998.

Lahvis, Sylvia Leistyna. "William Rush: Indian Trader," *Magazine Antiques* 156, no. 6 (December 1999): 846-53.

Lewis, Herbert J. "Panton, Leslie & Company." In *Encyclopedia of Alabama.* Last updated May 29, 2014. http://www.encyclopediaofalabama.org/article/h-3049.

M'Ferrin, John B. *History of Methodism in Tennessee: From the Year 1783 to 1804, Vol. 1.* Nashville, TN: Publishing House of the Methodist Episcopal Church, 1888.

McKenny, Thomas and James Hall. *History of the Indian Tribes of North America: with Biographical Sketches and Anecdotes of the Principal Chiefs. Embellished with One Hundred Portraits from the Indian Gallery in the War Department at Washington, Vol. II.* Philadelphia: D. Rice & Co., 1872.

Nairne, Captain Thomas. *Nairne's Muskhogean Journals: The 1708 Expedition to the Mississippi River.* Edited by Alexander Moore. Jackson: University of Mississippi Press, 1988.

O'Brien, Greg. *Choctaws in a Revolutionary Age, 1750-1830.* Lincoln: University of Nebraska Press, 2005.

———. *Pre-Removal Choctaw History: Exploring New Paths.* Norman: University of Oklahoma Press, 2015.

O'Donnell, James H., III. *Southern Indians in the American Revolution.* Knoxville: University of Tennessee Press, 1973.

Palmer, William. P., ed. *Calendar of Virginia State Papers and Other Manuscripts from January 1, 1782, to December 31, 1784.* Vol. 1 (1875), Vol. 3 (1883), Vol. 4 (1884) and Vol. 5.

Papers of the War Department, 1784 to 1800. Center for History and New Media. http://wardepartmentpapers.org.

Phelps, Dawson, ed. "Excerpts from the Journal of the Reverend Joseph Bullen, 1799 and 1800," *Journal of Mississippi History* 17 (October 1955).

Prucha, Frances P. *Indian Peace Medals in American History.* Madison: State Historical Society of Wisconsin, 1971.

Putman, A.W. *History of Middle Tennessee; Or, Life and Times of Gen. James Robertson.* Knoxville: University of Tennessee Press, 1971, reprint of 1859 edition.

Ray, Kristofer, ed. *Before the Volunteer State: New Thoughts on Early Tennessee, 1540-1800.* Knoxville: University of Tennessee Press, 2014.

Robertson, James. "Correspondence of General James Robertson," *American Historical Magazine,* nos. 1-4 (1896); nos. 1-4 (1897); nos. 1, 3-4 (1898); nos. 1-4 (1899); and nos. 1-3 (1900).

Rudd, Constance A. "Chickasaw National Recreation Area," *Encyclopedia of Oklahoma History and Culture,* www.okhistory.org.

Sargent, Winthrop. *Diary of Col. Winthrop Sargent: During the Campaign of MDCCXCI.* Georgia: Wormsloe, 1851.

Satz, Ronald N. *Tennessee's Indian Peoples: From White Contact to Removal, 1540-1840.* Knoxville: University of Tennessee Press, 1979.

Saunt, Claudio. *A New Order of Things: Property, Power, and the Transformation of the Creek Indians, 1733-1816.* Cambridge: Cambridge University Press, 1999.

Sessions, Ralph. "William Rush and The American Figurehead." *Magazine Antiques* 168, no. 5 (November 2005).

Smith, William Henry, ed. *The St. Clair Papers, Vol. II.* Cincinnati, OH: Robert Clarke & Co., 1882.

Stiggins, George. *Creek Indian History: A Historical Narrative of the Genealogy, Traditions, and Downfall of the Ispocoga or Creek Indian Tribe of Indians.* Edited by Virginia Pounds Brown. Birmingham: University of Alabama Press, 1989.

Storm, Colton, ed. "Up the Tennessee in 1790: The Report of Major John Doughty to the Secretary of War." *East Tennessee Historical Society Publications* 17 (1945): 119-32.

Swanton, John R. *The Indians of the Southeastern United States.* Washington, D.C.: United States Government Printing Office, 1946.

———. *Indian Tribes of the Lower Mississippi and Adjacent Coast of the Gulf of Mexico.* Bureau of American Ethnology, Bulletin 43, Smithsonian Institution. Washington, D.C.: Government Printing Office, 1911.

———. "Social and Religious Beliefs and Usages of the Chickasaw Indians." In *Forty-Fourth Annual Report of the Bureau of American Ethnology,* 173-273. Washington, D.C.: Government Printing Office, 1928.

Toomey, Michael. "State of Franklin." In *Tennessee Encyclopedia of History and Culture.* University of Tennessee Press, January 2010. http://www .tennesseeencyclopedia.net/entry.php?rec=509.

Verhoeven, Wil. *Americomania and the French Revolution Debate, 1789-1802.* Cambridge: Cambridge University Press, 2013.

Watson, John F. *Annals of Philadelphia and Pennsylvania Olden Time.* Vol. I (1850), and Vol. II (1844). Carlisle, MA: Applewood Books.

Weeks, Charles A. *Paths to a Middle Ground: The Diplomacy of Natchez, Boukfouka, Nogales, and San Fernando de las Barrancas, 1791-1795.* Tuscaloosa: University of Alabama Press, 2005.

Weeks, Terry. "James Robertson." In *Tennessee Encyclopedia of History and Culture.* University of Tennessee Press, January 2010. https://tennesseeencyclopedia .net/entry.php?rec=1137

Whitaker, A.P. "Alexander McGillivray, 1783-1789." *North Carolina Historical Review* 5, no. 2 (April 1928): 181-203.

———. "Spain and the Cherokee Indians, 1783-98." *North Carolina Historical Review* 4, no. 3 (1927): 252-69.

White, Kate. "John Chisholm, Soldier of Fortune," *Chronicles of Oklahoma* 8, no. 2 (June 1930): 233-39.

Williams, Samuel Cole. *Beginnings of West Tennessee in the Land of the Chickasaws, 1541-1841.* Johnson City, TN: Watauga Press, 1928.

———. *History of the Lost State of Franklin.* New York: Press of the Pioneers, 1933.

Windrow, J.E. "Collins D. Elliott and the Nashville Female Academy," *Tennessee Historical Magazine* 3 (1935): 74-106.

Winston, E.T. *Father Stuart and the Monroe Mission.* Meridian, MS: Press of Tell Farmer, 1927.

Winterbotham, Rev. William. *An Historical, Topographical and Statistical View of the United States, From the Earliest Period to the Present, Vol. III.* London: J. Ridgeway, Piccadilly, Sherwood and Co., 1819.

Woodridge, John, ed. *History of Nashville.* Nashville, TN: H.W. Crew, by the Publishing House of the Methodist Episcopal Church, 1890.

INDEX